WHO ARE WE?

D1651881

LEO SLOBODIN

outskirtspress
DENVER, COLORADO

To Karen for her love, inspiration, patience
and three wonderful children: Alan, David and Elise.

Contents

Introduction

What a piece of work is man! How noble in reason! How infinite in faculty! In form and moving how express and admirable! In action how like an angel! In apprehension how like a God! The beauty of the world! The paragon of animals!

– W. Shakespeare

AH, BUT MR. Shakespeare, that paragon of philosophers and playwrights, got it only half right in these deliberations. There is unfortunately another equally defining aspect to the human animal that does not resonate as well but which he thoroughly accounted for in his masterful plays.

What is the nature of man? An animal that has created and nurtured glorious music, beauteous visual art and design, enlightened literature, brilliant peaceful scientific discoveries and technological achievements, culinary masterpieces; endowed as it is with humor, pathos, morality, love, spiritual contemplation, delectation of the body, appreciation of the beauty of nature and thought and much more. And yet...

And yet unless you've been in a coma or space warp during your rational years you've no doubt become disheartened, perhaps desensitized, to the ceaseless daily reportage of the senseless mayhem that humans inflict on themselves: murders, warfare, terrorism, genocide, racketeering, the vast selling and consumption of addictive drugs, befouling the planet with growing hordes, crimes local and against humanity, along with greed, treachery, prejudice, hate, stupidity singly and en masse, deception - the list goes on. It is not localized. It is a worldwide affliction like a rampant incurable disease with seemingly no way to stop it. And surely, for evil to flourish and be tolerated, a rich bed of ignorance and stupidity (aka ignorance compounded) must abound together with a large dollop of dumbness. How else to explain the rise of Nazi Germany, its many predecessors and eventual successors? Strangely enough, evil behavior is not viewed by current society as a clinical, treatable ailment. It is simply accepted as a normal, perhaps undesirable, characteristic: chaff comes with the wheat.

We seem to be the only species on earth that fears none other than itself.

By all evidence we are the most gifted of earthly creatures yet at once the most destructive and deadly to all other life forms, to ourselves, and the planet at large.

Ancient Chinese philosophers seem to have

recognized this dichotomy within ourselves: a duo of opposing forces that sometimes become unbalanced which they called yin and yang. But are these "forces" contained within any given individual or are they somehow distributed among the human population at large bursting forth at some critical level of imbalance in unpredictable places, times, and forms? Experience tells us that individuals do not come in extremes: either a mystical state of rapturous enlightenment and morality on the one hand or the total embodiment of evil on the other. There are intermediate gradations, but many observed behavioral attitudes seem clustered near either extreme. After all, concert pianists rarely commit crimes against humanity (although some may disagree).

What is causing this unpredictable and mostly sorry state of human affairs? Why have we come to this?

After 8000 years or so of civilization, people can be forgiven for expecting that most of the possibilities for human experience have been exhausted and, therefore, nearly all problems have been dealt with innumerable times with well thought-out, readily known and available solutions. Or are we like squirrels condemned by our genes to endless repetition of life's functions but unable to learn significant insights from past generations so as to improve our lot? It is indeed frightening to contemplate how little we learn from generation to generation.

To what extent are people responsible, individually or collectively, for their actions? To what extent should people be held responsible for their behavior? Who is to assess their degree of guilt or innocence? By law? By religious or moral concepts? Can morality truly exist in a competitive society? Is survival a zero sum game in which some survive well but only at the expense of others?

Are we part of and witnessing a mutation of the human species into a sort of bifurcation of the path of human existence into good and evil directions? If so, which direction has the greater numbers now and why? Is goodness or evil the aberrant behavior? And which will eventually prevail? Of course, no human life is long enough to get more than a fleeting glimpse or momentary understanding of a multimillion-year biological phenomenon. But perhaps by examining our current ways of life together with those of our all-too-recent recorded historical past much as one would in trying to decipher the activities of people in a few photographs we might deduce some insights.

This book comprises a collection of essays by the author that examine human beginnings, societal motivations, education, politics, the justice system, the arts, spiritual yearnings, education, scientific pursuits, social interaction, economic systems, and the like as a means of understanding and describing who we are and thereby enable ourselves to assess and more confidently address the future.

Yet, can one who is a member of this species have the temerity to believe it is possible to fathom the essence of human value?

If indeed, as the popular saw has it, human nature will never change (until mutated perhaps), then we are condemned in perpetuity to live and deal with its frailties in a very costly struggle to survive. Walt Kelly's comic strip character, Pogo, succinctly stated the task before us: "We have found the enemy and he is us". Is it inevitable that the past is truly a preview of our future? Perhaps there is a possibility that goodness and evil can find a way of speaking to one another in the dim hope that the latter can be educated and redeemed. H. W. Longfellow believed "The wrong shall fail and the right prevail". We must work very patiently to achieve that or there will be no future.

CHAPTER 1

Starting Out: Are Our Genes Our Destiny?

GOOD OLD IMPONDERABLE mother- nature never intended that human beings be perfect in their conception or deeds. Humans are as faulty in these respects as all the other creatures that inhabit this orb. It may very well be that these imperfections promote, through a mutative process, what nature intended: the survival of the species. Beyond that, nature is sinless and humans are left to make their own moral destiny.

What forces are at work to produce in homo sapiens by far the widest range of disparate behavioral characteristics of all earthly creatures and when in our lives do such forces exert their greatest influence?

Most biological scientists agree that first and foremost, our genetic heritage, which has evolved over several million years and is the genome package given to us individually at conception, predisposes and defines what each of us is: a human animal with individual potential capabilities, traits, and temperament. An extremely important, but secondary, influence is the fostering provided to each child during the earliest months and years of life such as nourishment, love, language, information, discipline, education, preparation for life's struggles, etc. that ultimately shapes who we are and fleshes out each one's potential to a greater or lesser extent. However, no matter how well and caring this fostering may be done, it can never override the fundamental genetic essence of an individual -- as painting and decorating a house can never change its fundamental structure. However, it is not unreasonable to expect that, over the long haul, measured in millenia, our methods of child-care will affect in some way the genetic make-up of individuals. And it is the individual's characteristics we're concerned with here, not those of a population at large.

Babies are such a nice way to start humans. They are so cuddly and cute. Some say that they are born clear of mind but their character and understanding are thenceforth formed by the nurture of their culture. That is a facile way of saying that all newborns arrive with an identical tabula rasa upon which may be impressed the beauties and glory (as well as the detritus) of human heritage and all will be well at maturity. Unfortunately, historical evidence and personal experience tells us this is not necessarily so. If at birth receptivity to certain external stimuli is diminished, or the stimuli themselves are diminished, the emerging child and eventual adult may have difficulty surviving normally in today's world. Aside from possible careless or inadvertent exposure to environmental pollution, willful ingestion of harmful substances, improper or insufficient diet, or contraction of disease by the mother during pregnancy, the newborn is entirely the captive of its genes: the birthright of its existence. This consideration is non-specific to any group and entirely universal. It is the next step - that of parenting - that is most crucial to the outcome of the enterprise.

The most important and responsible task of parents vis-a-vis society or even civilization at large is the proper rearing of their offspring. Parenting consists fundamentally of protecting, nurturing, and teaching but parenting has always been and currently is haphazard at best. Mating is essentially a random process. There is little or no societal constraint on who mates with whom, the number of offspring they may bear (except in China lately), nor how these children shall be reared. In some cases, betrothals are set between families based on "good blood" or heritage or even good money. Worldwide, the poorest people are the most prolific and the most careless in mate selection and breeding. Indeed, a large number of children are born out of wedlock unintended, and ultimately abandoned. Yet society succeeds or declines directly as a function of the fulfillment of the parenting task. If that task is improperly done for whatever reason consistently through many generations, it is conceivable that the offspring of the Nth generation may acquire a degenerative quality that was most pronounced during the previous generations. As with widely observed, generationally reinforced, physical features of a clan, an ethnic group, or a race there is good reason to expect that certain mental attributes, which are, after all, also physical manifestations, should be reinforced too. For example, consistent multi-generational malnourishment possibly coupled with the promulgation of ignorance and hate may eventually genetically precondition a newborn that way prior to the first external stimulus. A preponderance of such occurrences can be disastrous for human civilization. Or perhaps not; Darwinian reasoning may say this is simply a survival technique. After all, there are seven billion of us now and counting despite all the mistakes. Nevertheless, one has to wonder why society so far has not generally seen fit to limit or license parenthood to only those couples predisposed by character and intelligence to bear children and care for them properly so they become an asset rather than a burden to society. Who can be the judge?

Good child care begins on the day of birth. No period of life is more important than its start. Focusing on a relatively brief period of time can lead to a whole lifetime of promise and benefit to the individual, family, and society. Although our biological gestation period may be only nine months, our intellectual, emotional and spiritual development lasts a lifetime. The brain at birth is a work in progress. Relatively few connections among its billions of cells have yet been established. Brain development research, pioneered by Dr. Ilg a half century ago, indicated that virtually all human vital neural connections are formed within the first few years of life. During those years, the brain begins to wire itself up at a furious pace, forming up to millions of synapses every second -- so quickly that the brain of a two-year-old is actually far more dense with neural connections than the brain of an adult. Within this brief initial period of synaptical "exuberance", the brain is especially sensitive to its environment. Many recent studies show the crucial role that responsive, sensitive and stimulating care plays in forming those synapses. Good, loving parental care at this stage is vital. For all we know, infancy may be an experimental research program and the parents are the lab rats. Has nature designed us to teach babies as much as it has designed babies to learn?

After three or so, that burst of activity seems to slow down, and our brain begins the long task of rationalizing its communications network, finding those connections which seem the most important, pruning others, or converting certain synapses to other uses. Most of this conversion, which is nearly complete by about age ten, likely occurs after a specific learning process, say toilet training or spoken language, is deemed, by our genetic code, to have been accomplished. The converted synapses are then devoted to more intellectual pursuits as learning history, science, etc. We see the results of such synapse activity when we observe that people who are forced to learn a second language in their teenage years and beyond always have a detectable accent which no amount of study or practice can eliminate. Noam Chomsky and Steven Pinker, both of M.I.T., have explained by their studies, that many of the synapses involved in learning a native language during the earliest years have been converted later to other uses and are no longer available for a second language. The same process pertains to instrumentalists, gymnasts, and the like: one must start at a very tender age, while the synapses are all there, to achieve the highest level of proficiency.

A bad care situation where a young child is inadequately loved, improperly supervised, understimulated for long stretches of time, or moved among ever-changing caregivers (does it take a village?) because of parental ineptitude or family breakdown may cause long term harm to a child's cognitive and emotional development. Contributing to this problem is the increased prevalence of mothers working or on career tracks for economic or social reasons (poverty or feminist movements?). A number of studies have shown that more than 80% of the children who got into trouble came from the poorest segment of the study samples. Breast-fed infants, who are usually indicative of loving care along with healthy mother's milk, and are generally smarter according to some studies, may soon become a rarity.

Could the costly, continuing increase in the U.S. prison population be partially related to inadequate maternal (and paternal) attention to offspring?

Moreover, if the way we live changes cyclically or at a rate quicker than a generation as with the modern acceleration of life, it may preclude parents from preparing their children sufficiently and properly for the new conditions the parents have not experienced (generation gap). Then you turn on the TV and, without careful, parental program supervision, a crud culture pours out and much prior constructive, mind-building efforts may come undone, tumbling down like a house of shards. Moreover, the ubiquitous Internet free-for-all is beginning to supplant television as a key mind bender for kids. No one knows what this will lead to. Also, it's anybody's guess what the results of child rearing by gay couples (or singles) will ultimately be. With increasing numbers openly attempting that today, it's an experiment in progress. Will this create more gay people than occur randomly as a natural, genetic process? And if so, so what?

Are there enough resources in the world, economic and otherwise, without restraint in mating and childbirth, to allow the nurturing of all children to their maximum potential so their productive lives will profit society at large and give each one the highest level of potential happiness? Improbable, and getting more so with each passing day.

Further study by Dr. Morris Massey of the University of Colorado some twenty five years ago determined, after much investigation, testing and analysis, that a person's basic personality, attitude and life-coping ability are well established and set by the age of ten. Afterward, though these characteristics may become more finely honed, they will not change throughout life and thus a person's approach and reaction to life's vissisitudes remains eminently predictable. These findings are covered in his book "You Are What You Were When" as well as videotapes of his lectures. On this basis, wouldn't it seem reasonable for parents and society at large to be extremely careful about what is taught to children and what they are exposed to by the media? And, a propos, if you have a hang-up in believing that personalities are well formed by ten, think again. How many times have you heard or said, "people never change"? Think of adult friends or relatives you knew well as early classmates or childhood chums and you'll quickly realize that certain funky personality traits of theirs and even handwriting hasn't materially changed through the years. As a matter of fact that's a basic way we recognize individuals.

In this context one cannot fail to acknowledge that among the factors that affect human behavior is familial birth order. This factor has been thoroughly researched over a period of 25 years by Frank Sulloway, a professor at MIT, and described in his book, "Born to Rebel". The findings contained in this book, with perhaps an homage to Darwin, are supported by a multivariate analysis of 3,890 scientists involving more than a million data points culled from 500 years of history and over 20,000 biographies. Sulloway finds first borns "more assertive, jealous, defensive, power hungry, conservative" while later borns are "more inclined to identify with the downtrodden, and to question the status quo to the point of becoming revolutionaries". These attitudes, a proxy for differences in age, power and privilege within a family system, are childhood survival techniques which are carried forward into adulthood as personality traits and eventual career paths and even voting patterns. In aggregate, such characteristics can conceivably affect the survival of the human species. This is a monumental addition to evolutionary psychology (though not yet universally accepted) which examines human behavior through the lens of Darwin wherein nature's diversity is a strategy that helps individuals minimize direct competition for scarce resources. In a family setting this diversity manifests itself as sibling rivalry during childhood in search for a family niche and later, a societal niche. There are millions of years of biology telling individuals how to get the most to maximize survival and thus fulfill the process of natural selection.

Can genes cope with morality? Is there such a thing as moral intelligence? Rustin McIntosh, a distinguished pediatrician, expressed it just that way in dealing with children some decades ago. Some were innately "good and kind", who thought of others, even extended themselves to others who were "smart" that way. Many, of course, were not. I suggest childhood is the time when we learn the morals that guide our lives, but it is our genes that determine our receptivity to this learning process. We grow morally as a consequence of learning how to deal with others, how to behave in this world, and being an attentive witness of grownup morality. Parents must start sending signals to their kids from day one. Children expand their horizons as they grow. Initially, they are intensely interested in themselves (self consciousness) and their feelings, then in a single person (mother), a room, house, others, a yard, neighborhood, town, country, and beyond. Certainly in elementary school, maybe as never before or ever afterward, the child becomes an intensely moral creature, quite interested in figuring out the reasons of this world - how and why things work, but also how and why he

or she should behave in various situations. Moral understanding forms character. Ralph Waldo Emerson once
said, "character is higher than intelligence". If we don't
teach morals to our children at a very young age, society
will eventually decay or implode into an uncontrollable,
chaotic, deadly morass: a Sodom and Gomorra past critical mass from which there is no sensible survival.

Finally, after all that, hormonal hell breaks loose at
puberty and all prior influence may be disowned even
including the existence of parents. (How were you created? I accumulated.) House, clothes, food, an allowance,
etc....I'm alive: I'm entitled to these by nature. Drugs,
sex, a little larceny: they'll never know. If genes and
earlier training aren't up to reining in these urges, no
parental influence or control at this stage and beyond is
possible. Adolescence itself is, after all, a form of tem-
porary insanity. Most make it to adulthood substantially
unscathed but some succumb to an unproductive life of
mayhem. So far medical science has not come up with a
cure for adolescence.

People may sometimes grow up depraved because as
young children they were deprived of love, inspiration,
discipline and the like. But what of the so-called incorri-
gible bad seed? ...the many cases where preconditioning
by a few capricious genes seems to preclude all or most
attempts at behavioral control and moral direction. Can
this be blamed on a bad care situation? At what point in
life and to what extent does a personality flaw become
recognizable by society as a dangerous malevolence
possibly treatable with pharmaceuticals? What can or

should we do about it? And when? Is such defect or malevolence contrary to or part of nature's survival game? Did the Nazis come to a realization that a Jewish heritage ("bad seed" in their minds) was fully genetic and there was no way, even with "proper training", around that impediment?

With the decoding of the human genome, we may be in for a lot of surprises vis-a-vis our present understanding of how our mind is created, booted up, and functions.

Not dealt with in this section are the effects of clinical mental problems, severe neglect, trauma (concussion) to the brain in early childhood, birth defects, etc., conditions where the cortical and subcortical areas never develop properly which affect both intelligence and emotional development, the effects of social upheaval brought about by revolutions, war, pestilence, and malnourishment. It is probable that malevolence or evil behavior might be brought about by any or all such circumstances.

Recently the concept of "memes" has been introduced to try to explain the rapid change of attitudes or ideas that are cascading around us at a pace far quicker than any genetic mutation or generational change can possibly explain or absorb. The science has been dubbed memetics. It involves cultural manipulation -- some would say brainwashing -- at the earliest ages to inculcate religion, hate, computer operation and function, forms of entertainment, new technologies (cell phones, MP3, rock music, IPod's etc.).

Ultimately, no matter what is written here, we will just have to learn to live with nuts and crackpots however discomforting and inconvenient and at times threatening and deadly they may be.

It's all in the beginin', the rest is fill in.

CHAPTER 2

Society's Devils

THE THEME OF crime and punishment runs like an unbroken thread through the fabric of human civilization. Not only lawyers, but philosophers, theologians and novelists as well, have grappled with the questions it raises and the problems it poses. On the one hand is the need of evidence to convict, on the other is the appropriateness and adequacy of the punishment. What is a suitable penalty to fit the degree of violence and the extent of damage done to victims? This is particularly poignant in the case of murder (or genocide) when life cannot be reinstated or compensated for. Who can establish the monetary value of life?

Should there be any punishment and if so, why? Is punishment as revenge necessary or useful? Should and can the punishment be stiff enough to deter future criminals? Is rehabilitation possible? Is public safety and security an issue? (Although at present, it seems to me the public passion for justice is quite boring and artificial....for neither life nor nature cares if justice is ever done or not.) Isn't all murder an insane act (at least psychologically speaking)? Is the concept of pleading legal insanity as a shield for execution crazy in itself? Are there real extenuating circumstances? Is crime preventable by providing more love, education, or police? What percentage of the population should be police to be sufficiently effective against crime? Who will police the police? Is the cost of prevention cheaper than the cost of apprehension? And ultimately, who is responsible for crime: the perpetrators, the parents, society at large, or a measure of all three? Regardless of choice, we all pay. This is certainly society's big overhead.

Experience seems to indicate that we have not reached critical mass with existing punishment for crimes in terms of eliminating or substantially reducing current crime or preventing future crime. Moreover, our criminal justice system today is so creaky and archaic – frequently more than a decade passes between apprehension and sentencing. Alan M. Slobodin (my son), a government lawyer in Washington, D.C., addressed this very issue in a solicited op-ed piece some years ago for USA Today entitled "Never mind causes; get after the criminals" cited in its entirety further on.

At mid-1998, jails and prisons in the United States held an estimated 1.8 million people according to a Bureau of Justice Statistics Report. At an estimated $30,000 yearly upkeep cost per prisoner, the direct aggregate cost to American taxpayers was in excess of $50 billion. Couple that with the ongoing construction costs of new prisons for an increasing felon population and that of the police and court system needed to apprehend and process them and I suspect we're looking at an overall public burden in excess of $200 billion every year and growing (that's close to $700 per U.S. resident), plus the pain and suffering of the victims and their families. One in every 155 persons in the USA is currently in prison. Should we accept this societal overhead as an inevitable consequence of human frailty or can criminality be reduced or even eliminated?

What pushes some people to commit heinous acts of crime? Of course, it's possible they engage in evil and mayhem simply for adventure and excitement with minimal concern about its effects. Is it the ready access of tools of the trade, i.e., guns? Exposure to violence in the mass media? Substance abuse? Social and economic inequality? To some, prison may be a step up from their street lives by providing a way to obtain good shelter and three squares a day. Any psychologist, sociologist, theologian, or philosopher will tell you it starts with the family's abdication of love and support for its offspring thus tossing that responsibility to the government which then must serve "in loco parentis" as the ultimate, underfunded babysitter and prison-builder. But even if families were perfect, would that really stop crime?

Historically, an overwhelming majority of violent felons continue to be young persons and getting younger, down to ages in the single digits. Maybe we need better high chairs and better high schools before they get to high courts....not to mention better parents. Should parents be held responsible for the bad acts of their offspring? To what extent....parental incarceration? Are we failing to provide adequate tuition to our young people? After all, the education of our youth is the foundation of our civilization. Society's behavioral expectations and punishments for certain activities should be explained to young children during their rational moments before they do something dumb or follow a path of crime.

Never mind 'causes'; get after the criminals

WASHINGTON – If we are going to stop violent crime, the last thing we need to be doing is spending money to come up with more excuses for criminal behavior. Trying to look for socioeconomic causes for violent criminal behavior is just another way of looking for excuses not to punish criminals. This is not only foolish but dangerous.

Looking for excuses denies the reality of making moral choices about right and wrong. When socioeconomic causes of violent crime are assumed, it follows that if criminals are not solely responsible for their actions, they don' deserve punishment.

The effect of this excuse-making is pernicious. This kind of thinking has led our criminal justice system to rely heavily on furloughs (a la Willie Horton), probation and parole, insanity defenses, plea bargaining and indeterminate sentences.

As carried out, our criminal justice system does not deter crime because:

- the time between arrest, conviction and punishment is considerable.
- the uncertainty of being caught and punished is great.
- the severity of punishment is too light to matter.

In short, violent crime is increasingly going unpunished. While reported crime rates have risen by more than 24% over the last decade, many convicted criminals serve only a small portion of their prison sentences or do not go to prison at all. Those convicted of violent crime typically serve only half their sentences in prison. Overcrowded prisons are turning into a revolving door of crime.

Worse yet, the criminal justice system is overwhelmed with a new, violent criminal who is casual in the commission of his crime. Today's criminals dismiss any suggestion that they ought to feel guilty about their behavior.

Why on earth would we want to continue down the road of not punishing violent criminals?

By not holding them to account, violent criminals sense weakness and a lack of resolve in our society.

That will only encourage violent criminals to commit more crime.

Violent crime is escalating not because we have failed to treat the criminal as a victim of some unknown socioeconomic cause but because we haven't cracked down hard enough.

We know there is little doubt that, under proper conditions, punishment deters. What is needed is to increase either the speed, certainty or the severity of punishment, or some combination of all three. We need to deploy our resources in this direction.

We are fighting a crime war in the USA, and the bad guys are winning. Preoccupation with the underlying socioeconomic causes of violent crime will only fly in the face of what needs to be done to murderers, rapists and other violent criminals.

Alan M. Slobodin

The editorial of the same issue of USA Today that ran the above item discussed criminal violence and is partially excerpted below:

Safety of your own home...friendly neighborhood... are cozy phrases that are being blasted into oblivion by violence. The mean streets have a way of following people, day and night, indoors and out.

- To a New York apartment where a sleeping 5 ½ month old baby was hit in the head by a stray bullet that tore through the bedroom wall. She is the sixth young child shot in 18 days in the city. Four of them are dead.
- To a Los Angeles Fourth of July celebration, where a 2 year old boy was in the line of fire during a drive-by shooting.
- To a Belleville, Ill., tavern, where a man fatally stabbed his estranged wife as horrified patrons watched.
- To a quiet Tulsa, Okla., neighborhood, where a 12 year old girl was tied up and set on fire by an unknown assailant.

Where do such unspeakable acts come from?

What explains the callousness that drives kids to label stray-bullet victims "mushrooms"? Why are some people so quick to act on anger? Why are they so slow to feel remorse?

Unquestionably, we need swift and sure justice to protect society from murderous creeps. When a person commits murder and this action is proven beyond a doubt – to object to putting that murderer to death requires a saintliness I do not possess. They must pay for their crimes. But then what? Even as this is being written new heinous crimes continue to be committed without pause or surcease such as those within various school-yards around the country where the bodies of innocent children lay strewn about, shot by their own classmates. How many mournful speeches and eulogies and burial mounds, --and for children—heart shaped balloons, poems, and stuffed animals staring blankly into space, will it take for us to address and stop the most serious crime imaginable—murder? (And ultimately war and genocide?)

And what about those who are wrongfully incarcerated through the actions of overeager prosecutors with weak evidence and strong egos? It is probable that a small but significant percentage of prisoners are behind bars needlessly, some awaiting execution. Governor George Ryan of Illinois in 2002 declared an indefinite moratorium on executions until the "flawed" state justice system could be trusted. According to lawyer-writer Scott Turow, detailed reviews and cross studies showed "no evidence that killing a killer makes murder less likely"—but it provides solace to some of the victim's relatives. He also maintained that "moral ambiguity exists where truth is never the whole truth and justice is often a point of view".

Obviously the threat of incarceration or even execution has never been, is not now, and will probably never be, a successful means of stopping crime. Thousands of years of experience around the globe confirm this. It may reduce it by some as yet indeterminate rate but not eliminate it. Certainly, prevention by retention does curtail some mayhem by current criminals, but seems to have no deterrent effect on future prospects. Even instant execution and the application of Hammurabi's law (an eye for an eye, etc.) in some countries does not seem to have eradicated crime there. It does, however, seem to satisfy the understandable demand for revenge. The true root causes of crime have yet to be found. This doesn't mean that extensive research is not being done in this field. For example, a recent study published in the Archives of General Psychiatry claimed that test results support the hypothesis that maternal smoking during pregnancy is related to increasing rates of crime in adult offspring. Interesting, but hardly practical in terms of crime control. But note that this study looks for a physiological cause before birth rather than familial or governmental inadequacy.

There are some who believe that with sufficient moral development and inculcation of society's behavioral expectations in early childhood serious crime can be eliminated. Like trying to eliminate driving accidents by teaching youngsters "the rules of the road" before getting a driver's license. It undoubtedly does some good but young drivers are nonetheless still the main cause of automobile accidents.

So where do we go from here? Are the causes of crime completely the result of our culture? Are we getting close to fathoming the workings of the human mind so as to predict criminal intent? The public, I'm sure, fully appreciates the fact that the mind controls the body that perpetrates crime yet the public today would probably rebel at any attempt to medically alter the mind of a convicted felon to a personality of benign acquiescence and then release that individual as cured, completely without penance or punishment. Or is malevolence a human instinct or frailty built into our DNA for survival from which we have no recourse? Or are we at a point now when, with the recent success of the genome project, we can envision this problem being dealt with medically on a genetic basis? Even if we stumble upon the genetic cause for human proclivity to crime, would the public be receptive in time to medical alterations of the genome of potential or actual criminals? As adults? As teenagers? As young children? Would such activity be seen as eugenics redux? Would courts allow or sanction it? Would we then turn into cookie-cutter, pleasant humans with possibly a reduced mutative process? What if the genes that cause crime were found to be embedded in the gene group responsible for our better selves, then what?

I bet within a few generations hence, much of this genetic approach will be accepted and will become settled medical and legal procedure and practice and that prisons and executions will then be viewed as quaint as guillotines and medieval dungeons. Meanwhile, in today's world, constrained as we are by the lack of a fundamental understanding of the criminal mind, we must suffer the detritus of crime: the great cost and uncertainty of apprehension, an expensive criminal justice system and inadequate levels of punishment, uncertainty of convictions, a rapidly growing prison population of incorrigibles (many imprisoned for life), the loss of life, the pain and suffering of victims and their families, the constant reappraisal of parental and societal obligations, and ultimately the effect on our social and moral conscience.

And now since the tragedy of 9/11, the war on terrorism may have superseded the war on urban crime, but the arguments are the same. Do you want to be free or safe? Do you attack root causes or crack down on offenders? Should you be worried about why people do evil or only how? Is it prudent, or is it bleeding heart, to try to understand criminals or terrorists—or put another way, to ask, "why do they hate us?

CHAPTER 3

Between Heaven and Hell

*"You have to be taught before it's too late
Before you are six or seven or eight,
to hate all the people your relatives hate.
You have to be carefully taught,
you have to be carefully taught."*

– from *"South Pacific"* by Richard Rodgers
and Oscar Hammerstein

NO GROUP, TRIBE, nor race of people has yet been, or is likely to be, discovered that did not have a form of religion, special deities, or shamans no matter how isolated from other peoples. This universal human trait bears looking into indeed. Some may regard such organized religion as something produced by nature since no human society has been found without one. Undoubtedly, at some early time in human existence, many occurrences in life could not be understood, rationally explained, or controlled, such as creation, illness, death, good or bad hunting and harvests, extended drought, storms, earthquakes, simply contemplating the awesomeness of nature, good or bad luck, and the apparent existence of good and evil in different individuals: a sort of chaotic immorality. Life's uncontrollable vicissitudes had to be attributed to a mysterious, higher, all-powerful "divine" entity (a Causeless Cause: the ultimate secret, God) which oversaw and governed the activities and well being of humans and perhaps all other creatures and things in the universe as well. This belief is held to this very day.

Such an entity, either comprising a single deity, a God, or multiple deities, a pantheon of Gods, was developed over millennia either as an unseen imaginary being or iconized in various ways. This entity was ascribed powers, and/or the embodiment of power and morals beyond human attainment because it became evident that people would not accept the guidance of a flawed human in moral and spiritual aspects of life. I believe it was David Ben Gurion who declared that there must be a being, intangible, indefinable, even unimaginable, but something infinitely superior to all we know and are capable of conceiving. If a man arose and declared to the people what was right and wrong, he would be regarded as a dictator or a pompous ass. But if that someone was said to be of divine origin or could communicate with or represent a divine entity yet offered the same message he would be regarded as a great leader and savior, usually well after his death. Around that time we were all sacrificing goats to some rain deity and receiving stone tablets on mountain tops. And religions then, though different for different peoples, generally espoused the endless cyclic nature of life: the sun rises and sets, storms come and go, birds repeat migrations, the tides move up and down, there is birth and death, birth and death and so on and on. Time was perceived as a wheel, spinning ceaselessly, never altering its course. (Some Asian religions still practice that belief with the use of prayer wheels). People rarely moved any significant distance from their place of birth. Until, as T. Cahill put it in his book *The Gifts of the Jews*, "Abraham hears the voice of (his) God speaking the unexpected words 'go forth'; he then leaves Sumer in the third millennium and meanders his way to Canaan following God's dictum. This simple step showed that man could affect his destiny in a progressive manner--plant crops and invent new things. Thus the concept of an unknown (non-cyclic) future takes hold and Western civilization is born". As we know, this has not been an unmitigated blessing.

Religion is many things. Among its aspects are symbols, practices, rituals, and scriptures along with mythologies to rationalize the unrationalizable, but at the core of all religions is a set of beliefs (not logical or reasoned scientific certainties) about creation, moral guidance and the nature, meaning and purpose of life. In fact, if a divine entity is indeed involved in the creation of the universe and all its elements, as most religions espouse, that entity is so fearsome as to be beyond any human entreaty for our solace, or comfort, or the redemption that would come of our being brought into

His secret. Moreover, such divinity is ahistorical. In fact, it may be that God and religion are incompatible.

Unfortunately, historical evidence has not illuminated organized religion in a kindly light. It's anyone's guess how many thousands of people were slaughtered in ritual sacrifice in ancient times under the most barbaric circumstances to placate Gods created by the self-same people (the Maya, for example). In 1642 England descended into a civil war that was based solely upon religious opinions. For centuries religious leaders have used their power to promote and enhance the welfare of aristocracy and themselves by extracting coins and toil from the myriad poor to grow and sustain their institutions and hierarchy. Priests pray, the people pay. They have always promulgated the exclusivity of their specific faith over all others to the detriment of peace and life. Religious institutions have always feared scientific progress (Galileo) and logical thinking (education—evolution vs. creationism for example) as destructive influences in their attempt to control people's minds and destiny. Moreover, any social or economic amelioration of the masses is and has been cause for concern by many religious institutions because it tends to diminish the depth of piety of the people.

In a constant tug of war between sets of ideas promulgated by faith-based (religious) and logic-based (secular) groups, there seems to be no intellectual common ground whereby these ideas can be debated and compromise achieved with common acceptable goals to which both sides can subscribe. This intractability will end when faith is overtaken by secular education. Are we confusing personal religion, ethics and morality with organized religion?

Where ignorance reigns, organized religion flourishes.

Nonetheless, most organized religions, in attempting to cope with the mysteries of life and death and to comfort the soul, offer a set of precepts which, if actually followed, do provide a good basis for the development of a moral society. Generally, these precepts say we should make choices between good and evil by using an ethical system not invented by man but by a divine creator that is a framework of truth and moral guidance through which we can find peace and deliverance from despair. Unfortunately, these moral principles were and are inconsistently followed, even by the very people who professed and wrote them down, their descendents, the preachers who espouse them, and their followers. Moreover, religion tends to splinter itself into ever smaller denominations perhaps down to the tribal level, to a family, and if the trend continues, eventually to solitary individuals, each with his or her personal "comfort" religion, or none at all.

All this to accommodate minute variations of principle or understanding. Moslems have their Sunnis, Shiites, Salafists, Hashemites, Alawites plus others; Asians their Buddhist, Shinto, Hindu, Moslem beliefs, and more; Christians their Catholic, Eastern, and myriad protestant churches: Presbyterian, Methodist, Episcopelian, Congregationalists, United Church of Christ, Lutheran, Church of the Latter Day Saints (Mormons), Seventh Day

Adventists, Church of the Nazarene, Pentacostal, Baptist, Anabaptist, Unitarian, Jehovah's Witnesses and countless derivatives. Then there are Shakerism, and others. Jews have three main branches at last count: Orthodox (including Satmar and Lubovich), Conservative, and Reform, plus a number of other varieties such as Jews for Jesus, and Messianic Jews. And on and on. These are only some of the major organized religions of today. Then there are those of us who just believe in money. One must also acknowledge atheism (a belief in disbelief) where the idea that a benign God created us and watches over us is somewhere between a fairy story and a bad joke; agnosticism (nothing provable or unprovable) and religious zealot groups such as Davidians of Waco, Jonestown, Heavens Gate, Shinrico, and others that believe(d) in separatism, murder or mass suicide: clear demonstrations of the vulnerability of ignorant minds. Many earlier religions, such as that of the Maya referred to earlier, dealt in continuing blood sacrifice.

So many religions, intransigent in their orthodoxy, necessarily imply a narrow and precisely defined sphere of persons who qualify as properly religious in each religion. One consequence of such detailed specification of religious legitimacy is identification of a number of persons and groups as religiously illegitimate. That leads to the belief that a given religion has an exclusive patent on religious "truth". Such fanatic intolerance of contrary creeds by this kind of religious self-righteousness has been proved in blood throughout history. In this spirit Moslems slew, and were slain by, the hated infidel. It inspired the racks and stakes of the Inquisition, the St. Bartholomew's Day massacre, the burning of convents, the Holocaust during World War II, and more—the record is so long, brutal, and well known that it need not be recounted. In regard to the Holocaust, James Carroll, a former priest, claims in his book *Constantine's Sword* that Christianity is to blame for persecution of the Jews throughout Europe and has set the stage and allowed, encouraged, and at times chartered the foulest of abuses and murder. By tapping into over a millennium of church-inspired hatred of the Jews, Hitler made the church an accomplice and effective sword bearer in the Holocaust, history's worst crime.

Humans seem to have the uncanny ability of self delusion: praying for deliverance from evil while simultaneously waging war and killing. Every warring faction says God is on their side. More wars were (are) fought, more people persecuted, tortured and killed in the name of religion than for any other reason.

Religions seem intolerant of each other, in some cases, like anti-matter. Beliefs are converted to feelings which are then converted to action. A prime example of this is the seething cauldron called the Middle East: thousands of years of implacable hate and still counting. By this time, after many generations, the hate must surely comprise some genetic ration: a hereditary obligation to hate. This may be why, since education and understanding of religions other than their own is deemed pointless by people living there, some of their leaders seem to have embarked on a genocidal crusade as the only means in their view, of solving their religion's problems. There are other examples of this throughout the world today. Ireland (Catholic-Protestant), Bosnia and Kosovo (Moslem-Christian), Armenia-Azerbaijan (Moslem-Christian), Rwanda-Burundi (Hutu-Tutsi), Chechnya-Russia (Moslem-Orthodox Russian Christian), India-Pakistan (Hindu-Moslem), the world vs. the Kurds, and many more. Many of these current religious rivalries may be cast in economic and ethnic terms and vice versa. When religion and ideology embrace, beware.

Looking through a lifetime lens one has to wonder--can this folly be intentional by a creator? We have somehow not quite learned to deal with the concept of God without turning faith into a weapon. If religion has so far proven so deadly, why do people follow it? Can morals and ethics be instilled without religion? Is religion simply a bastion of rituals and traditions? In any case no particular religion has so far demonstrated its superiority to any of the others in having any affect whatsoever over human nature, which is equally pervasive throughout all religions.

The basis of religion is faith. The very essence of faith is a belief in the existence of something that can't be proven. Theologians maintain that belief is something beyond proof. So, naturally everyone believes their faith is the "right" one. This makes all faiths equally valid (or invalid), giving no one the right to claim any religious superiority. So—shouldn't all faiths be practiced in a spirit of religious tolerance?

God, after all, exists only as a human concept: no

other creature in this world has any awareness of a lordly existence. Is it possible that God needs us humans as much as we need Him? Were human beings created by God out of a sense of vanity to have someone for show and tell? Who created whom? These are some things to ponder.

Though religious institutions have done a creditable job maintaining traditions and instilling family values, they have unfortunately and simultaneously created mutually assured separation of their diverse adherents. In essence, we in the U.S. (representing a microcosm of the world's people and their indigenous faiths) are currently leading parallel ethnic/religious lives with little or no social interaction among groups with perhaps only the slightest possibility of ethnic convergence at some far horizon. Our main social interaction today is in educational institutions and at our workplaces but a major difference compared to the world at large is that we live under a common secular law with minimal religious distractions and that is a very significant force for learning how to live together.

Moral issues became the mainstay of religions because neither science nor the quotidian business of life seemed capable of answering questions like: Why am I here? What is the meaning of life? What do I do with my life? How do I deal with the future? How can I tell right from wrong? Is there a right or wrong? Or good or evil? Religion can be a meditative process to help one address such things. As a scientist, Stephen J. Gould addressed the moral issues best: "Science does not and cannot, in principle, find answers to moral questions or supply information as input to a moral decision. I win my right to engage in moral issues by my membership in Homo sapiens--a right vested in absolutely every human being who has ever graced this earth, and a responsibility for all who are able. If we ever grasped this deepest sense of a truly universal community then Isaiah's vision could be realized, and our human wolves would dwell in peace with the lambs, for "they shall not hurt or destroy in all my holy mountain". We are freighted with heritage, both biological and cultural, that grants us capacity both for infinite sweetness and unspeakable evil. What is morality but the struggle to harness the first and suppress the second".

Albert Einstein wrote: It seems to me that the idea of a personal God is an anthropomorphic concept which I cannot take seriously. I feel also not able to imagine some will or goal outside the human sphere. My views are near to those of Spinoza: admiration for the beauty of and belief in the logical simplicity of the order and harmony which I can grasp humbly and only imperfectly. I believe we have to content ourselves with our imperfect knowledge and understanding and treat values and moral obligations as a purely human problem—the most important of all human problems.

To Socrates is attributed the following wisdom: "philosophy begins when religion ends, just as by analogy chemistry begins when alchemy runs out, and astronomy takes the place of astrology".

*One wonders what Darwin would have thought

about the seeming 'naturalness' of religion. Well, he did address that issue fearing his writings would be the end of his reputation by saying " the discovery of natural laws should exalt our notion of the power of the omniscient creator".

Religion, whether divinely inspired or not, is surely one of the great enduring inventions of man.

And the hate and killing continue…

CHAPTER 4

An Experiment in Socialism

IT HAS BEEN remarked recently by esteemed historians and journalists that the so-called G.I. Bill of 1944 was the greatest piece of legislation passed by any congress in U.S. history. This measure, a.k.a. Public Law 346 a.k.a. the Servicemen's Readjustment Act of June 22, 1944, passed by one vote (senator John Gibson of Georgia) and was signed into law by President Franklin Delano Roosevelt with little fanfare.

Did congress realize at the time that it was enacting the most socialistic law ever in the sense that, although its proximate purpose was to provide chiefly free education, low mortgage rates and business loans for returning war veterans, it literally transformed our society and way of life for everyone in the U.S.A. to this very day, seven decades later? Some may believe that the Social Security Act is a close contender for first place as socialistic law, but lets not waste energy debating the difference between excellent and best. Whereas the intent of Social

Security is to provide an economic parachute for seniors and thereby release money into the economy, the G.I. Bill gave young people education, monetary support, and a home for their new families thus enabling them to create technical innovation, new industries, and new attitudes heretofore unrealized which far surpass the effects of Social Security. It pulled the G.I.s up by their combat bootstraps and put them among the most educated and financially well-off generations in U.S. history.

Within 2 years college campuses were flooded with over 2 million young World War II veterans (including 60,000 women and 70,000 African Americans) who had never in their lives expected to be there. At a cost of $5.5 billion the G.I. Bill turned out 450,000 engineers, 240,000 accountants, 238,000 teachers, 91,000 scientists, 67,000 doctors, 17,000 writers and editors and thousands of other professionals. The cost, which included tuition, all fees and books, and subsistence allowance amounted to an investment in each student of about $4500. Teachers agreed at the time that the G.I.s, being about 23 years old as entering freshmen, applied themselves more diligently than they had experienced with 18-year-olds. Thus, it would seem that several years of public service or military service (if they so choose) should be a pre-college requirement and certainly would be beneficial as a maturing process. When the initial program ended in 1956, close to 8 million of the nation's veterans had gone to college or received job training.

Passage of this one law gave to the U.S. economy its biggest boon ever and it's still continuing. The return on this capitalist investment has been so great as to be beyond monetary measure. A whole generation flourished and even returning veterans from subsequent wars received equivalent benefits. On that basis it would seem that the greatest national economic benefit derives from government investment in people, particularly young people in the form of direct support of education, health and economic opportunity rather than from possible downward seepage of benefits that may result from tax breaks for the wealthy. So why not adopt this as a continuing national policy?

When, oh when, will we learn?

CHAPTER 5

All God's Chillun

IN THE BEGINNING God created the white slaveholder and the black slave. And behold there were many of them. For several hundred years in America they lived side by side, slaveholder and slaves, completely separate, segregated, parallel lives with no intersection save for the toil and the not infrequent sexual dalliances by the slaveholder. The slaves were kept subordinated and subjugated in wretched poverty, totally uneducated, ignorant, and illiterate, their dark skin color an unmistakable mark of social position.

And it came to pass that such condition, despised by the non-slaveholders, could not persist and a great war was fought and many lives were lost to retain the unity of the nation and, as a result, the slaves finally attained their long sought freedom. Disappointingly, few whites came to help the former slaves who, being unfamiliar with the ways of life in their new-found freedom, found it extremely difficult to make it on their own. Many succeeded despite persistent prejudice, segregation, lynching, ostracism and general treatment as social pariahs for more than a century after emancipation, but most did not. All this despite the pronouncement in the Declaration of Independence that "all men are created equal", a phrase that is a central argument for ending slavery and bringing blacks into true citizenship. Nevertheless, they and their progeny exhibited great creativity and continue so in many fields especially in the development of musical forms (jazz), dance, and showed exemplary prowess in sports, all of which we enjoy today.

Their almost revolutionary fervor to remove the chains of multi-decade intolerance by the white community was impelled by many black leaders including Martin Luther King to a level of clamor that finally prompted the enactment of a host of civil rights legislative initiatives including desegregation of public facilities and schools, busing to lily-white schools, equal opportunity employment, open college enrollment, affirmative action for college enrollment, favored treatment of black businesses by government entities and much more. Implementation of these initiatives was a massive 40-year process.

Imagine! Just the concept of having to enact legislation expressly for the benefit of a given ethnic group in a polyglot society to force that society to accept and treat that group as co-equals with the remainder must tell one a lot about the weakness or strength of that society and human nature, depending on your point of view.

Every adult human being on this planet is aware of the wicked injustice of slavery. Yet slavery is not an endowment of nature: it is a sporadic human predilection surely derived from the days of conquest and subjugation of peoples millenia before written records. Of course, we continue to be eternal slaves to hunger and just staying alive but we should never be anyone's chattel.

It is interesting to contemplate that since slavery and segregation in America were engendered almost entirely by the British whites that inhabited this country (colonies or nation) in the South prior to the Civil War, they must be held fully accountable for such shameful and degrading behavior. [To understand how widespread slavery was in the South, accept the fact that there was nearly one black slave for every white person. Just prior to the civil war, the population of the south was 9 million of which 5 million were whites and 4 million were black slaves. At that time, the population of the North was 21 million including a very small but significant population of slaves. Hence, the total population of the country then was about 30 million (not counting native Americans.) To be sure, most of the British whites in the north, to their credit, opposed black slavery; hence the war. The churches supported either side with equal fervor depending on church location. Yet, despite the war and the passage of more than a century and five generations, to this very day a substantial portion of Anglo-Saxon progeny as well as others still bear intolerant attitudes in this regard. Couple them with the skin-heads, residual Ku Klux Klans, white supremacy and aryan race promoters and you have an evil brew indeed.]

It is not unrealistic to believe that the spread and maturation of eastern European peoples and their culture in America, following the massive immigration of their forebears to these shores in the latter part of the 19th century and early 20th century to escape their forms of intolerance and economic deprivation, may have blunted black prejudice and enabled the passage of civil rights legislation in the 1960's.

The blacks were now left with the task of meeting the challenge of attaining the intellectual achievements of the white world that predominates in this country. That means coming to grips with the need to improve their education to a competitive level with whites so as to advance economically and politically. The gates of higher education were now suddenly thrust open with few external barriers to achieving their highest expectations: "be what you can be" to quote the army's recruitment slogan. Unfortunately, they were totally unprepared, certainly initially, with the prospect of open enrollment newly available to them and sitting side by side with white students. Earlier, their educational achievements, developed in inadequate and segregated institutions, were well hidden and, for the most part, unmeasured in relative or absolute terms. (Sadly, many black students, particularly those from an inner city environment, looked upon a good educational drive as kowtowing to whites rather than as a means of escape from their squalid surroundings.)

In entering colleges geared to white levels of study and marking, the woeful limits of black learning were glaringly exposed as never before. "The tests were not in our (ghetto) language, how can we succeed?" Then the marking system was changed to a lower standard at many institutions so more blacks could pass courses. Curricula were diluted to the point that Shakespeare became optional and Toni Morrison mandatory and students could study comic books under the rubric of "cultural studies". Educators began looking at the sufficiency of preparation for higher learning of black students provided by elementary and secondary schools and found that greatly wanting. Forget science and math. These schools were sending black students to college who required remedial reading and writing instruction. Although considerably improved over several decades, these inadequacies still persist.

This is a serious matter since the social progress of Black-Americans is being inordinately delayed by the sluggishness of their educational achievements. Is it failing schools or failing education? Or failing students? The definition of what's "failing" and the word itself is critical to solving one of education's thorniest problems: the stubborn gap between white students and their black and even Hispanic counterparts. Can the bar on student achievement be raised equally for all ethnic groups? Can consistent national standards be set for all educational institutions to ensure adequately educated citizens?

At present, there is no denying a statistical or preponderant lack of interest in education by blacks as shown by countless tests and evaluations over decades across the nation of curricula, teaching methods, bussing to mostly white schools, increased funding and so on. Like denying that the sun causes daylight, the necessity of breathing to sustain life, and the existence of gravity. There is also no denying the horrendous effects of many years of intense racial prejudice, illiteracy, and economic barriers on a people's psychological outlook. Nonetheless, there seems to be an inability by the black community itself to fundamentally understand and define their educational problem directly: if you can't state the problem, you will never find a solution. But I'm sure at some point they will, at which time there will be great reason to celebrate. After all, nearly all anthropologists agree there are really no measurable intellectual differences between human races on this planet.

Meanwhile America will continue its struggle to come to terms with the legacy of slavery. It will be as nuanced as the many shades of "black" that the community embodies as a result of natural amalgamation and the racial enlightenment of time. We will build a more egalitarian, multiracial society and blacks will join whites as equal citizens of the United States. Let's hope it is soon.

From time to time a few well-known personalities from the black community step forward and acknowledge the sluggishness of blacks in moving ahead in the educational and economic world. In the 1990's the reverend Jesse Jackson in speeches at schools throughout the nation berated black students for laziness and not pulling themselves educationally ahead by the bootstraps now that they had the opportunity. "Go for it!" he intoned to little avail. In 2006 the famous entertainer Bill Cosby spared no anger when he wrote and widely distributed an essay entitled "Can't Blame White People" that totally unraveled the NAACP. I include it below in its entirety because of its relevancy.

Can't Blame White People
By Bill Cosby

They're standing on the corner and they can't speak English.

I can't even talk the way these people talk:

Why you ain't,

Where you is,

What he drive,

Where he stay,

Where he work,

Who you be...

And I blamed the kid until I heard the mother talk.

And then I heard the father talk.

Everybody knows it's important to speak English...

Except these knuckleheads.

Mushmouth is what they speak!

You can't be a doctor with that kind of crap coming out of your mouth.

In fact you will never get any kind of job making a decent living.

People marched and were hit in the face with rocks to get an education,

and now we've got these knuckleheads throwing that all away.

The lower economic people are not holding up their end in this deal.

These people are not parenting.

They are buying things for kids. $500 sneakers for what?

And they won't spend $200 for Hooked on Phonics.

I am talking about these people who cry when their son is

standing there in an orange suit.

Where were you when he was 2?

Where were you when he was 12?

Where were you when he was 18?

And, how come you didn't know that he had a pistol?

And where is the father?

Or who is his father?

People putting their clothes on backward:

Isn't that a sign of something gone wrong?

People with their hats on backward,

Pants down around the crack,

Isn't that a sign of something?

They're walking around with their nasty underwear showing,

and holding onto their pants to keep them from falling to the ground!

Or are you waiting for Jesus to pull his pants up?

Isn't it a sign of something when she has her dress

all the way up to her panty line,

and got all types of needle piercings going through her body?

What part of Africa did this come from?

We are not Africans;

They don't know a thing about Africa.

With names like Shaniqua, Taliqua and Mohammed and all of

that crap, and all of them are in jail.

Brown or black versus the Board of Education is no longer

the white person's problem.

We have got to take the neighborhood back.

People used to be ashamed.

Today a woman has eight children with eight different 'husbands' –

Or men or whatever you call them now.

We have millionaire football players who cannot read.

We have million-dollar basketball players who can't write two paragraphs.

We as black folks have to do a better job.

Someone working at Wal-Mart with seven kids saying...you are hurting us.

We have to start holding each other to a higher standard.

We cannot blame the white people any longer.

It is not for media or anyone of this time anymore to say
whether I'm right or wrong.

It is time, ladies and gentlemen, to look at the numbers.

Fifty percent of our children are dropping out of high school.

Sixty percent of the incarcerated males happen to be illiterate.

There's a correlation.

Tell the media to stop asking me what I think about people who don't believe what I'm saying or feel that I'm too harsh or feel that I'm just running
my mouth because I'm old.

Seventy percent of the teenagers pregnant happen to be
African American girls.

Don't ask me to soften my message.

CHAPTER **6**

How Can You Buy or Sell the Earth?

WE ARE OF the land and sea. Make no mistake: whether you are reaping corn, catching fish, or reading this in a 12th floor condo, realize that we are forever tied to these elements. But can we say we truly own them? City folk and others full of their cosmopolitan sophistication may think they are beyond or have escaped that consideration, but it is not so. The necessities for their very existence are fully imported. The water they imbibe comes from water cascading down from the mountains or sucked up from aquifers, food is trucked in from farms or taken from the sea, power is derived from earthly matter. Who owns the air? Who owns the fresh water? Who owns the sea? Who can own the very land we stand on? Is everything up for profit? Our custodianship of our host planet has so far been tantamount to desecration.

In addressing this subject I came across a message written to a United States president by an American Indian chief. The message, written (or dictated) in 1854 by chief Sealth (Seattle) of the Dwamish tribe was addressed to President Franklin Pierce who offered to buy two million acres of Indian land in the Northwest where the Dwamish lived. It has been described as the most beautiful and prophetic statement on the environment ever made. It is presented here in its entirety.

"The Great Chief in Washington sends word that he wishes to buy our land. The Great Chief also sends us words of friendship and good will. This is kind of him, since we know he has little need of our friendship in return. But we will consider your offer.

How can you buy or sell the sky, the warmth of the land? The idea is strange to us. If we do not own the freshness of the air and the sparkle of the water, how can you buy them?

Every part of this earth is sacred to my people. Every shining pine needle, every sandy shore, every mist in the dark woods, every clearing, and every humming insect is holy in the memory and experience of my people. The sap which courses through the trees carries the memory of the red man. So, when the Great Chief in Washington sends word that he wishes to buy our land, he asks much of us....

This we know: All things are connected. Whatever befalls the earth befalls the sons of the earth. Man did not weave the web of life; he is merely a strand in it. Whatever he does to the web, he does to himself. But we will consider your offer to go to the reservation you have for my people. We will live apart, and in peace.

One thing we know, which the white man may one

day discover --- our God is the same God. You may think now that you own Him as you wish to own our land; but you cannot.

He is the God of man; and his compassion is the same for the red man and the white. The earth is precious to Him and to harm the earth is to heap contempt on its creator. The whites too shall pass; perhaps sooner than all other tribes. Continue to contaminate your bed, and you will one night suffocate in your own waste.

But in your perishing you will shine brightly, fired by the strength of the God who brought you to this and for some special purpose gave you dominion over this land and the red man. That destiny is a mystery to us, for we do not understand when the buffalo are all slaughtered, the wild horses are tamed, and the view of the ripe hills blotted by talking wires. Where is the thicket? Gone. Where is the eagle? Gone. And what is it to say goodbye to the swift pony and the hunt? The end of living and the beginning of survival. So we will consider your offer to buy the land.

If we agree, it will be to secure the reservation you have promised. There, perhaps, we may live out our brief days as we wish. When the last red man has vanished from the earth, and his memory is only a shadow of a cloud moving across the prairie, these shores and forests will still hold the spirits of my people. For they love this earth as a newborn loves its mother's heartbeat. So, if we sell our land, love it as we've loved it. Care for it as we've cared for it. Hold in your mind the memory of the land as it is when you take it. And preserve it for your children, and love it… as God loves us all. One thing we know, our God is the same God. This earth is precious to Him. Even the white man cannot be exempt from the common destiny. We may be brothers after all."

CHAPTER **7**

Too Many Neighbors

IN JANUARY 2003, I was moved to write an open letter to then Governor James E. McGreevey of New Jersey decrying the incredible population growth around me that I was witnessing first hand. Having lived in the same house in Holmdel for over 45 years, the 9-fold growth in the area is truly eye-popping.

The first obvious assault one observes is the vast increase in traffic congestion prompting an increase in the number of local traffic lights from 0 to 12. Now we have at least 6 shopping malls and growing in the area. Where once private wells sufficed for good, clean drinking water, we are now serviced by township-wide water pipe systems provided by companies for a substantial monthly fee. North Holmdel, between Routes 35 and 36 has people living cheek-to-jowl in town houses and minute parcels of land made possible, I suppose, by some zoning board oversight, stupidity or developer pressure. This had the result of quickly overloading our schools with many new students and thereby shooting property taxes through the roof. There doesn't seem to be any escape from this while still alive.

Hence the open letter, which was published as a guest column in local newspapers. This letter is presented below.

Dear Governor McGreevey,

The blight of growth is spreading over New Jersey like fungus. Where once we were and continue to term ourselves the Garden State, our soils are being rapidly smothered under homes, warehouses and concrete, our watersheds constantly in danger of abuse or loss due to insistent suburban sprawl. If not contained or diminished it will rapidly morph into urban sprawl, then high rise apartment sprawl, followed predictably soon by commercial sprawl, and finally industrial sprawl clear across the state which by then will resemble a Manhattanesque nightmare. All this growth will place unimaginable strains on our collective psyche and the state infrastructure which must deal with the masses of new highways, mass transportation systems, crime, schools, and acquisition of life necessities that will be needed. We are now at a decisive point in New Jersey history where this impending catastrophe must be stopped. And that connot be done if left to the vagaries of the 500 or so towns in the state, each with its own home rule mentality.

I commend you for your concern and initiatives toward reigning in this sprawl. But your good intentions in this regard will be to no avail and will certainly be doomed to failure without the passage of necessary legislation to curtail unlimited population growth. Such a law must be strong, unassailable, enforceable and define a maximum population for New Jersey at a level sustainable by the natural resources of the state and to a large extent, the attitudes of current New Jersey residents. Barring that, we will be overcome by river-to-ocean masses of people and concrete where all food and water are imported and all waste exported. That may be what the developers and builders dream about but I doubt that's what you, the legislature and the people envision for the future.

Even the past administration came to the realization that preservation of farmland was important to the future of New Jersey as a way to curtail untrammeled growth. It set aside a budget to eventually buy up to a million or so acres thus removing that land from potential development. Study after study shows that open lands, farms and forests require less infrastructure, fewer roads, water, sewer systems and schools and actually create a tax surplus based on their benefits to society. Today most towns realize the futility of chasing after new ratables to pay for the folly of the old. Lately, developers and local politicians have latched onto the oxymoron "smart growth" as a way to enshroud new development from logical appraisal by the public. Smart growth works if you are a developer. But if you are a taxpayer, a homeowner, a small business owner, a worker, blue or white collar, more people means more taxes for all, old timers and newcomers alike. At some point you're going to be crowded by growth and paying for the discomfort.

I'm sure you must be well aware that if this sprawl is not immediately checked by action at the state level, a critical point will be reached in the very near future when there will not be sufficient funds in the treasuries of the state and all the counties and townships in New Jersey to stop it. Then how will you pay to acquire any remaining expensive land for public use and pay the necessary legal fees? If you think your budgetary woes are intractable now, do nothing about sprawl and they will become insuperable later as in California now. To be sure, there will be great howls of displeasure by large landholders that any growth restriction will diminish the value of their land and reduce the profits they could otherwise make selling to developers. However, there comes a time when the benefit to a single individual must be subordinated to the benefit of the society in which that individual lives. That time is now.

So I urge you, with all due respect, to become the anti-sprawl flag-bearer and lead the legislature in passing the very necessary law for population containment so that invasive sprawl can be curtailed for the benefit of our children, grandchildren and ultimately all New Jerseyans.

CHAPTER **8**

Why Tax Residential Property?

Property tax is a virulent form of home-icide

—L.S.

[THE FOLLOWING IS based on a speech I gave at the February 2004 public meeting of Holmdel's CILU (Citizens for Informed Land Use) organization. To avoid the scent of political suasion, I gave the talk as a private citizen rather than as president (which I was then) of the non-partisan CILU that had no stated tax policy.]

For many years I've been bothered, as I am sure many of you have been, by the concept of the taxation of residential property by municipalities. How did this arise and why do we accept this as a viable way of life? Why are we doing this to ourselves? Can and should something be done to diminish or eliminate it? Of course, this discussion will be of little or no concern to those who do not pay such tax but for the rest of us it is vital.

How many here believe they own property in Holmdel? Raise hands. False! The township owns all the property. If you don't believe me, don't pay your property tax for a couple of quarters and see who really owns "your" property. Don't pay it for a year and you're out of here. Sound like a familiar kind of extortion? In a way it is. Generally speaking, townships are essentially an agglomeration of private properties in a given area but the townships seem to treat them as if they were township property.

The usual concept of property ownership means you buy something—say, a bicycle, a book, a lawnmower— pay for it once and henceforth it's yours to keep. Not if it's real estate. For that, you generally buy it during your younger years and, aside from the mortgage, pay taxes in perpetuity for the privilege of ownership to the township (and county) in which it is located. That payment is not trivial: for a piece of land I own without a house on it I have so far paid to Holmdel township in the form of property tax 20 times the acquisition price of that land! In essence, you are forced to buy the property (assets) you already own over and over again.

How did we come to this sad state of affairs where we are reduced to taxing our own assets in the form of home and land in order to retain them? It's like taxing down your savings account principle as well as interest so as to stay solvent a while longer. It's like chopping off pieces of body extremities to feed the body to stay alive for a while longer. Only *income* and real estate devoted to *creating income*, i.e., businesses, should be subject to taxation. Only the aggregate *income* (not assets) of this country, which represents a measure of our Gross Domestic Product should be subject to taxation as a form of investment in ourselves and a means of maintaining or improving our ability to produce next year's GDP. But residential property produces nothing, it is simply a measure of assets. So why tax it?

Our property taxation system is derived from the archaic European custom of taxing income-producing, private property such as farmland, forests, waterways, mines, and the like as tribute by the lords to the king (chief lord) for protection against foreign and other threats. Then and through the early part of the 20th century, the quantity and quality of these assets were a good measure of the owner's likely income. It even provided an incentive to use the assets in a most productive way so as to enable tax payment and to provide a profitable livelihood.

In that tradition, the framers of the U.S. constitution included a provision in it that only men who owned land could vote in an election process. And presumably that meant they could vote for or against certain taxes (the basis of our revolution) through their representatives. Years later that provision was rescinded by amendment in favor, eventually, of universal suffrage which included no-land owners. So now income, excise, and sales taxation are accomplished at the federal and state levels. On the other hand, the taxation of property, income-producing or *not*, is accomplished solely by municipalities and counties, yet there are no words in the U.S. constitution that authorize or direct such tax collection. The New Jersey constitution, however, does.

During the course of the industrial revolution, taxable income-producing assets shifted substantially away from natural resources, such as farms, to commercial facilities. Family farms, which were and are a measure of potential income, became smaller and the farmhouse, which was a minor item on a large farm, assumed taxable significance on a much smaller farm. Moreover, a significant portion of the tax money collected was diverted to the schoolhouse as a separate entity from town hall. Today the farm has totally disappeared from the residence but, predictably, the taxes have not, even though the residence is non-income producing. The ultimate example of that is a condo or townhouse where you can barely get a lawnmower around it. Yet the owner pays property tax. This tax represents a major and growing bite out of the income of an average homeowner. The simple schoolhouse has now become the educational system that demands an overwhelming portion of the residential property tax.

As you are all well aware, today an average of 65% of the residential property tax collected by every town and county in the state goes to pay for our children's education. In 2003, it was 64% of the joint taxes alone. Why should that portion of the residential property tax devoted to public education be collected on the basis of property size or value (which bears no relationship whatever to educational need) rather than on the number of children a family sends to the township school system? And with increasing population density, Local governing bodies are forced to seek more property tax ratables to cover the cost of educating more students as well as to pay the cost of more infrastructure. This is a never-ending spiral toward disaster.

Taxing residential property is no different than taxing the principal in your bank account (in addition to taxing your interest). Politicians would be laughed out of office or worse if they proposed taxing your account principal, yet that's what they are doing to the residential property you think you own, and we are meekly accepting that concept. (I'm not talking about taxing home sales profit, which is properly an income tax).

Moreover, the taxing of non-income producing residential property encourages intense, unlimited build-out in a futile attempt by townships to chase after new ratables to pay for the folly of the old. The townships have only recently come to that realization as well as the recognition that build-out without surcease will lead to uncontained sprawl with its attendant problems and eventually to a Manhattanesque nightmare.

Our current level of residential property tax has become an unbearable burden for most homeowners in the state. Particularly hard hit are the retired and elderly among us who have spent a working lifetime paying off their home mortgages only to find their yearly property tax has risen to a level which exceeds that mortgage by a substantial level in many cases. And they send no children to public schools. It ill behooves young parents to sup at the table of the elderly to pay for the education of their children. In Holmdel today, approximately 40% of educational costs are borne by seniors.

In my view, the taxation of non-income produc-ing residential property to support public education should be abolished in favor of incorporating that tax into the personal and commercial income and other taxes collected by the state and federal governments. This transfers the tax base to where it belongs. Only income-producing property should be subject to local taxation. Michigan does this totally and California and Pennsylvania, partially.

A slow realization of the archaic, insidious nature of residential property taxation is occurring on the part of many residents and state officials in New Jersey. This is evidenced by the property tax relief actions state offi-cials have so far taken: the enactment of the Homestead Rebate Law a decade ago and, more recently, the en-eactment of the New Jersey Saver Rebate Program under which a small portion of property tax is replaced with state funds derived substantially from income tax. These were great starts.

Although such attempts at tax relief are laudable, I'm sure you realize the legislature was only chipping away at the fringes of the high tax rate (New Jerseyans pay the highest residential property tax in the nation. Statewide, property taxes rose 7% in 2002, the largest one year jump in a decade) rather than directly addressing the solution: residential property tax should not exist as an income source to pay for public education. That cost should be borne by the state with money derived from private and commercial income, sales and excise taxes. Residential property tax money should only be used to support local township administrative and police needs.

The funding of our children's public education by the state would not obviate the concept of home rule. Rather, in keeping with current law, the state board sets standards for educational requirements and accountability, teacher training and pensions, school building design requirements, and additionally, the state provides yearly education subsidies to each town.

So completing the education picture with full state funding would not be a major transition from what we have today. And if some towns want to add a few locally funded trinkets of their own over and above state requirements, why not? Local school boards would, as now, still manage their schools following state requirements.

Many serious, thoughtful people and organizations are advocating the tax principle I am enunciating tonight. Recently, a number of organizations and imminently, the legislature, are espousing a constitutional convention favored by the League of Women Voters, to address property tax relief or repeal.

To paraphrase a famous speech, I had a dream that one day in the near future government at all levels will be run at a profit instead of a loss as it is today and citizens will no longer have to pay asset taxes as a kind of cover charge for the privilege of residence. Nationwide we must learn to live within our means called the Gross Domestic Product as a measure of our aggregate yearly income. Taxing assets merely withers away repeatedly that which we have produced in the past and gives us a false sense of economic well-being and leads eventually to the next step of borrowing from the future to pay for what we want today.

> Postscript: After the property tax money is taken from you, the benefits you personally receive from the township for that money are not necessarily proportional to what you paid. That is, the township's taxpayers get an exactly equal bargain from the township regardless of their individual property tax burden. For example: police protection, road maintenance, snow removal, library facilities, common ordinances, open spaces, recreational facilities, parks and, of course, education are equally available to all. The collection is capitalistic, the service, socialistic. Does political clout in town hall depend on how much property tax you pay? Should it?

CHAPTER **9**

Equality of What?

IT SHOULD BE understood that men and women have always had equal, important but different roles in society. These roles are not readily interchangeable no matter how we may strive to do so. Men simply cannot bear children and without children humanity will, of course, quickly cease to exist.

Unfortunately, men have seen fit to give themselves preferential treatment because in their view, men's duty to family and society defined by working and fighting for familial and ethnic survival was the highest priority. (Some think maybe it still is). That mindset had the unfortunate consequence of seeming to relegate women to secondary roles in society: to disenfranchised chattel as women rightly see it.

Unfortunately too, for women to attain their concept of exact equality (from one of superiority, according to George Bernard Shaw) entails taking on men's roles without or with minimal change in their own. Few men seem to want the reverse for themselves. Women have always worked diligently beside their men in the fields, managed households, and up to the near past, borne many children in the hope that some would survive to care for them in old age. (The wealthy aristocracy has no place in this discussion). For reasons I am unable to fathom, women were excluded from higher education, banking services, voting in governmental elections or holding office, and even today in Muslim countries (where the accepted dress is a ghostlike chador, burka or the like) and India, they are ostracized if they remain single and are regarded as mere chattel. In China, where the birth rate is strictly limited, female babies are sometimes disposed of in favor of males. The twentieth century changed all that in the western countries as a result of the lengthy struggles of the women's movements as well as further education for all.

Today, however, the law of unintended consequences has caused some of the leaders of various women's movements to rethink some of their "successes" particularly in the workplace. By getting so many women to replace men in the workplace as well as the military (now that brawn is much less needed due to technological innovation), the available workforce has effectively doubled as far as employers are concerned causing the wages of all to be halved which in turn makes it mandatory for both the husband and wife at the middle-class level and below to work simultaneously to pay their bills which, predictably, were not cut in half. Hell for children and possibly for society at large, heaven for controlling inflation. And the women are now stranded with heavier work loads than ever. That's progress?

CHAPTER **10**

A Nice Big Brother

If men were angels, we wouldn't need a government.

– James Madison

CIVILIZATION HAS ADVANCED now to the point where human population seems to have distributed itself neatly into various groups around the world called nations, each with its own independent government and territory. (Religion, ethnicity and native cultures muddy this water a bit but the existence of nations cannot be denied.) By and large the governments and territories are fairly stable these days with a few nasty hiccups here and there. In most cases the people in the various nations were given or have chosen forms of governments that seem to congregate about a central theme wherein a controlling entity, as opposed to anarchy, is deemed advantageous to maintain order and economic stability and which additionally provides planning, guidance, some protection, and a sense of purpose and belonging (nationality, citizenship). So with all the varied forms of government and leadership that abound, it is informative to consider what the priorities of a good government ought to be especially in the United States which somehow deems itself the ultimate example.

Abraham Lincoln came close to defining it simply with the somewhat socialistic closing words of his Gettysburg address (which, with respect, I somewhat modified): "….government of ALL the people, by ALL the people, and for ALL the people….". I think good government should be concerned with:

1. Stabilizing population
2. Protecting the environment
3. Assuring an adequate supply of energy
4. Assuring the availability of sufficient food and water
5. Protecting its people from foreign aggression and terrorism
6. Assuring good health care for all its people
7. Providing economic stability via a federal banking system and regulation
8. Assuring that adequate education is equally available to all
9. Assuring provision of the best up-to-date transportation systems
10. Providing adequate police and a good criminal justice system
11. Establishing foreign policy and supporting the United Nations

12. Assuring freedom of speech (with caveats): the voice of the people must be heard
13. Promotion of technological research
14. Promotion and encouragement of the arts
15. Provision of good and adequate recreational areas and parks
16. Provision of technical control of communication media
17. Staying out of religious affairs
18. Assuring the best hi-tech and honest voting procedures
19. Controlling and licensing all non-military guns
20. Assuring that all elected government officials are chosen through a democratic process by the people
21. Establishing and empowering a national bill of rights for all citizens
22. Adherence to a constitution and laws
23. Creating and Maintaining a National Budget.

Is this agenda conservative or liberal? It is neither. It simply states the salient concerns of a viable and stable national government designed to give its people the best chance for long term survival and enjoyment without too many bumps along the way. Some thoughts about these concerns follow.

1. Stabilizing Population

Population restraint is the sine qua non of all subsequent concerns. Worldwide, the population is currently exploding at a rate equivalent to seven New York Cities or about 60,000,000 people every year. Without self-constraint we are (over)breeding ourselves to extinction. If people or governments fail to contain population growth, nature itself will cull the herd by disease, pestilence, starvation and, eventually, climate. Alternatively, this may be accomplished by revolution, terrorism and warfare. We are at that point now. This is not late breaking news. The innovative thought here regarding population growth is the inclusion of government as a guiding instrument in containing the number of its inhabitants to a steady state but dynamic, manageable size relative to its natural resources and applicable technology so as.to provide and ensure a good quality of life. The resources of this entire planet simply cannot sustain the existing and growing hordes in equal, acceptable comfort for all; it does so now for a lucky, select few at the expense and tolerance of the vast majority. China is currently the lead (perhaps the only) torch bearer here in recognizing and promulgating population constraint. Yet today we are on a collision course between our human compassion to preserve all human life by deterring birth control and by using our latest technological medical advances to control and eliminate various diseases versus nature's normally restrictive means. If population growth is not contained now, the end result will not be a pretty picture.

2. Protecting the Environment

To satisfy the needs of all, and indeed, the pleasures of many, this planet, our only hospitable home in the universe, is being ravaged by humans at an unprecedented rate perhaps to the point of irreversibility within a time frame those alive now can contemplate. It seems inconceivable that reasonably intelligent people would inflict harm on themselves and their offspring by disregarding the warning signs evident to our senses and those issued by our scientists. As I write this, I have the distinct gut feeling that I may be too late in addressing the unfolding environmental catastrophe that is currently engulfing us all. It is far worse than terrorism because of its insidious nature: by the time you become personally aware of it, it is too late to respond in practical terms to do you any good. But better said before dead! Recently, The United Nations issued a report summarizing more than 1000 pages of research conducted by some 700 scientists about the effects of rapid climate change brought about for the most part by the extensive burning of fossil fuels over the past 100 or so years and the likely future changes to be expected by continuing this activity.

The fastest way to reduce carbon emissions: don't have more than two children. Although the impact is high, the feel-good factor is very low. Face it, overpopulation is the biggest factor contributing to greenhouse gases, but nobody likes to point that out. As stated in my first concern above, if we don't reduce our population now nature will do it for us, whether we like it or not. Will we be able to adapt or are we just another soon-to-fail genetic experiment?

Scientists predict that global temperatures could rise by 10 degrees in this century which in turn would engender the melting of Alpine glaciers, produce coast-al flooding that could drown the entire state of Florida and many sea islands, reduce grain yields due to high temperatures, incur droughts, increase storm surges, increase the ranges of diseases like malaria, dengue fever and Lyme. There's much more. So who's listening? Are SUV owners listening? Do we have to have a Swiss cheese earth from drilling for crude? Where will we get sufficient potable water? We are losing quality water-sheds at alarming rates and in the United States, state and federal governments are failing to act to save them. At present, only a few percent of the earth's water is considered potable. Crop irrigation in the midwest is rapidly depleting the Oglalla aquifer. Clean, life-sustaining air is at a premium in congested areas around the globe. We seem incapable of addressing these problems singly or as private corporations. Only elected governmental entities, with the people's needs in mind, have the clout to enforce the action required for global environmental protection. But they must act now.

3. Assuring an Adequate Supply of Energy

Modern national economies demand energy in huge gulps to sustain and allow the growth of industries, the means of transportation, as well as residential/commer-cial heating and cooling that have been developed in order to create these very economies. Like drug addicts, we seem incapable of foregoing or significantly reduc-ing the use of fossil fuels to generate this energy although we have had the technological capability of doing so for

years. This capability comes in many forms: from readily available wind and solar power, to dams, hydrogen
fuel cells (whose waste is water), rechargeable electric
battery-operated vehicles, hybrid vehicles (gasoline-
electric combinations), ethanol-gasoline combinations,
nuclear fission (whose waste is radioactive and hence
needs to be buried deeply for many years), nuclear
fission with breeder reactors (less radioactive waste), nuclear fusion including the Tokamak reactor (whose waste
is non-radioactive), and others yet to come. Aside from
nuclear fusion, these energy sources are currently economically viable. The Tokamak reactor, an international
effort supported by China, Russia, Japan, the U.S. and
other countries, is currently under construction in southern France with a turn-on date currently set for 2019.
Unfortunately, within the United States, research in nuclear fusion as the Tokamak, which holds the promise of
being an almost limitless power source (it uses sea water derivatives deuterium and tritium), has been nearly
halted by congress either due to lack of funds, or fear
of political revenge by companies that deal in fossil fuels. Developed countries can either conserve petroleum,
drill for more with indifference to the environment, or
fight wars: their choice. The longer they wait the fewer
will be their options. This is where a strong government
serving the people is needed to direct conservation and
ultimately the creation, efficient utilization, and maintenance of a stable energy supply to undergird a strong
economy.

4. Assuring the Availability of Sufficient Food and Water

It would seem to be an elementary understanding that for people to live comfortably they must have adequate supplies of food and water. But the planet and, of course, the U.S. are finite in size which tend to limit, at some point, the availability of these necessities. We have so far been able to stave off spottily a good deal of starvation and thirst on the globe by technological advances (high yield seeds, expensive desalinization plants) and economical forms of food distribution from have to have not areas. This rearrangement of food and water supplies cannot go on indefinitely and it is doubtful that humankind and other creatures can mutate quickly enough to survive without food and water. This is definitely a zero sum game: the wealthy can afford to buy these resources from anywhere in the world at the direct expense of those who can't. With uncertain climate and weather, starvation at any time in various areas of the world will be bugging us for years to come. For the blessed or cursed, the future looks like tall buildings and scattered, preserved farmland, the ratio of which will ultimately have to be controlled by governmental entities.

5. Protecting Its People from Foreign Aggression and Terrorism

On September 11, 2001 the United States was attacked by Islamic terrorists at the twin towers of the World Trade center in New York City and at the Pentagon in Washington, D.C. Over 3000 innocent people were killed in the buildings and in the several aircraft that struck them including one airliner that crashed in Pennsylvania. All the airplanes were high-jacked by 19 highly trained men of Saudi Arabian origin. These occurrences were surely acts of perfidy and must be dealt with in kind. One can keen and remonstrate over such horror and its causes but a federal military force and domestic security services to curtail and prevent such acts in the future are our only useful near term responses. Only a national government can respond adequately to internal and external aggression. At the very least, these attacks demonstrate as no flood of words can, the need for a strong, well-trained federal military establishment to protect and provide all necessary security for its people.

6.   Assuring Good Health for All Its People

Try running a company with sick employees and see how long it lasts. Now try to keep a country going for the long pull with an unhealthy population and see how that ends up. Even a dimwit will tell you that's a recipe for disaster. Maintaining the health of every person and indeed the public at large to the best extent possible is an important national priority and responsibility. Today there are only seven or so means of maintaining general good health:

- good and adequate diet
- adequate exercise
- no smoking and very limited drinking (of alcoholic beverages)
- periodic health examinations

- early diagnoses and intervention
- treatment with pharmaceuticals
- surgical intervention.

It can always be expected that there will be a small percentage of the general population cursed with various genetic disorders which do not respond to the palliations listed above. These people must be cared for out of compassion and, hence, they form the basis of a necessary economic cost burden we must all agree to share alike for each other as an overhead expense that may be as high as 15% of GDP. (In the United States in 2004, we spent somewhere around 15.4% of GDP). Here, in a sense, we are our brothers' keepers. Failing that, we are looking directly in the face of triage and eventually euthanasia.

In assuring the health of its populace, national government must assume the responsibility for:

- Educating people about the importance of maintaining good health on a preventive basis
- Dealing with contagious public diseases
- Providing adequate vaccines
- Assuring adequate supplies and quality of pharmaceuticals
- Dealing with health care provision and cost
- Assuring adequate quality of medical care by professionals
- Furnishing managed care vs. managed cost
- Stopping the sale and use of tobacco and illicit

drugs. (This action alone can probably chop our $1 trillion yearly health care cost by 40% if we can muster the political will to do it.)

Can there be such a thing as competition in necessities like health care as opposed to competition in luxuries in a free marketplace? Although not specifically stated in the U.S. constitution (yet), only a federal government responding to the people's needs can be trusted to supervise the health-care market and thereby protect the health of all its citizens. (This is already an accomplished fact in many countries around the world). A free marketplace whose main concern is profit cannot be depended on or be expected to fulfill that need.

7. Providing Economic Stability via a Federal Banking System and Regulation

Economic stability gives government and its people the ability to plan a predictable long-term future. Without that stability, a totally free, unregulated market will fall prey to chaotic cyclical swings in prices, purchasing power, out-of-control inflation, inadequate wages, speculation and spastic global trade. Under those conditions it would be difficult, if not impossible, to establish consistent, long term interest rates needed for investment, or to allow people and industry to plan and save adequately for future needs or even determine how much to invest or save. There are many examples of such folly. No society or nation can function for long under those circumstances. In the United States the

Federal Reserve Banking System serves to partially control or attenuate instability. Other means available to the government are business regulatory measures, price and wage controls, plus the ability to tax and collect duties. Under our current free-market based capitalistic system, there is a continual reappraisal of the extent of such controls usually based on political pressures (unfortunately) rather than valid economic principles. But few would argue against the necessity of some control. That control, for maintenance of economic stability, at whatever level, is the government's responsibility.

8. Assuring That Adequate Education Is Equally Available to All

Education is the foundation, spirit, and pulse of human civilization. It's what keeps us from wallowing in the muck and mire with the beasts by giving us the ability to communicate complex thoughts, preserve some thoughts through writing, learn new things not preprogrammed into our psyche, create and enjoy arts, and live fruitfully together under common law. Long ago Thomas Jefferson said a democracy can only survive with an informed electorate. He was right on target, of course, but I hope he meant that not necessarily in a political sense but broadly, in an academic or "liberal arts" sense. It is of paramount importance to assure that all citizens have equal access to as much education as they can handle. And as G.K.Chesterton, the well known philosopher-writer pointed out, "Education is simply the soul of a society as it passes from one generation to another".

More education for more people translates into a higher standard of living. It makes no sense economically or politically to restrain or curtail the ability of an individual to achieve his highest intellectual capability by denying or limiting education by virtue of unaffordability or unavailability. The best investment a nation can make for the biggest payback is in the education of its people. (See chapter 4, *An Experiment in Socialism,* which discusses the benefits of the 1944 G.I. Bill, a huge, first time investment by the federal government in advancing the education of returning war veterans. It's still paying off.) Apparently it's a difficult lesson to learn. Government at all levels must promote and instill, by all means of communication at its disposal, the value of education as a key way for a person to become better as a citizen, as a breadwinner, and to enhance the development and progress of one's country. An educated populace usually builds intellectually on itself; that is, educational achievement improves generationally. It directly increases the GDP thereby allowing more people to get more education. Call it "common wisdom squared".

Public education in the U.S. is a comparatively recent phenomenon. A preliminary form was established by the Pilgrims in the mid 1600s in New England mainly to teach children and adults just enough to read the bible. But the attempt withered and by the middle of the eighteenth century, private education in the colonies had become the norm. By 1790 Jefferson believed that education should be under the control of the government, free from religious biases, and available to all people irrespective of their status in society. But it was only after much political, economic, and religious upheavals in the early 1800s that the first compulsory public school laws were enacted by Massachusetts and New York in 1852-3. By 1918 all states had such laws. And those were for elementary schools only. Believe it or not, Secondary (or high) schools came of age just during the 1900s. From 1900 to 1996 the percentage of teenagers who graduated from high school increased from about 6% to about 85%.

In today's political and educational climate in the United States, education of people can best be achieved in a multi-tiered system geared to student ages, vocational needs ie., matching skills to available jobs and needs, higher learning through college, and further advanced education for the truly gifted. This must be addressed at all levels of government: federal, state and local. The first tier, K through 12, requires the adoption of national minimal standards of curricula, testing and evaluation, coupled with substantial federal funding to make sure children are at least adequately versed in reading, writing, and mathematics. The curricula must have sufficient flexibility to change with the advent of new advancements in understanding and technology over time. It should be capable of dealing with a normally wide range of student intellectual capabilities and behaviors. Abnormal children must be graciously dealt with by specially trained teachers in special education centers purposely designed for such need. Certainly, education at the first tier should be neutral and untainted by political or religious beliefs. Those topics should be reserved for home or church.

At the second tier (as well as at the higher levels of the first), the skills taught should at least bear a reasonably close relationship to the needs of the marketplace for economic reasons. There will always be a lively, on-going debate regarding precise subject material in different areas of the country as history unfolds. This debate must quickly resolve topics such as adequacy of language skills, arts and science content, sufficient preparation for higher education, demographics, special education needs, sports, cost, teacher training sufficiency, plant requirements, acquisition of teaching equipment etc. Details of educational principles and methods to accomplish all this are beyond the scope of this section.

The third tier would provide advanced college education at or beyond the graduate level for the exceptionally gifted who will become tomorrow's professionals, researchers and leaders. These students must be assured that their study and talents will be rewarded with jobs and placement either in private or public sectors. They should not have to be confronted with cheaper foreign competition engendered by industrial globalization being promoted by our government these days.

As with health care, we must establish, as a closely-knit society, the amount of money that we are willing to invest to assure that an appropriate universal education is provided so as to maintain and advance our well being. I estimate the funding priority to be equivalent to our yearly defense budget. It may seem high but it is necessary. This funding should be viewed as a profitable public investment that increases the GDP rather than as another "welfare" expenditure.

It seems to me that the immense uncontrollable cost of private college education today has degraded to what it was in the nineteenth century and before: an elitist system mainly favoring those who can pay outlandish fees for entry into a political power network. Education at any institution must be sufficiently funded by federal and state sources available in that region and certainly not by local property taxes. As our educational understanding and methods improve, education will evolve into a smooth uninterrupted fully funded public system from start to finish.

9. Assuring the Provision of the Best Up-to-Date Transportation Systems

To a nation, its transportation system is akin to a body's vascular system and its blood flow. The blood must reach all body parts equally and adequately under many conditions to sustain life and "good health". A single good heart and vascular system see to that. Since all modes of transportation are interrelated in their coverage of a nation's needs, the idea that a nation's transportation system should not and cannot be efficiently managed under a single federal auspice relative to private enterprise (with its inevitable multiple points of control) is a grandmothers' tale of long standing professed by the American transportation industry.

Nearly every country in Europe is proud of its nationally-run on-time, high-speed, comfortable railroad and air services. Even in the United States privately run airlines look to the government (FAA) for establishing flight rules and regulations as well as standards for equipment to keep them flying safely. Likewise, railroads look to government at any level for subsidies, while automakers keep pressing for more and better highways (at everyone else's expense), least regulation of safety, air pollution and engine efficiency, as well as availability of fuel at any price limited only by what the public will bear and the presence of the federal Department of Transportation and its National Highway Traffic Safety Administration. Additionally, safety of our waterways and adequate maintenance (levees, dredging and the fleet itself including the Merchant Marine) is a high federal priority.

Left to their "druthers", railroads and airlines would seek "whatever the traffic will bear" fares, the ancient nostrum of the RR's; run tracks and routes only to the most populous areas to maximize profits mostly via freight rather than passenger traffic, and safety would be a distant concern measured on a cost basis for repair or replacement.

Responsibilities of a dedicated government agency must include:

- Setting standards and safety requirements for all modes of transportation systems
- Overseeing the design, construction and maintenance of bridges and roads

- Controlling cost for affordability
- The use and continual funding and update of the latest proven technology
- Leading the way for the most environmentally friendly applicable technology.

10. Providing Adequate Police and a Good Criminal Justice System

It is interesting to contemplate that humans need such a system to protect themselves from themselves by themselves and are willing to pay the high cost of maintaining it rather than disgorging its need and cause from society simply by sensible behavior. Consider Chapter 2, Society's Devil's. Is there any kind of logic that can explain why people commit mayhem and tolerate it to the tune of about $100 billion annually involving an army of police, prison guards, lawyers and judges, with over 2,000,000 persons behind bars in the United States and more being committed to prisons daily? Whether poverty, plain dishonesty, greed, insanity, ignorance, availability of weapons, use of and dealing in illicit drugs, prostitution, lack of good education,or other failings are the causes—select any or all from the list and/or add some—the results are a staggering burden to society.

For as long as human society exists, behavioral perfection will never be attained but it certainly can be improved from what it is to a less devastating level by increased intervention in child rearing, education and eventually, medical treatment in the not-too-distant future.

Until then we need laws and enforcement thereof, most of which currently exist, covering apprehension and detention for varieties of malfeasance, recompense for monetary damage, and much else that are well within the purview of governmental responsibility. This function cannot and should not be handled or discharged by private commercial enterprises whose sole interest is, of necessity, profit.

11. Establishing Foreign Policy and Supporting the United Nations

All countries on this planet must engage in the interchange of trade, people, environmental concerns and ideas as well as agreements on borders and areas of activity by generally accepted means to enable a peaceful and fruitful co-existence. These conditions require the establishment of constantly evolving foreign policies to maintain fruitful and stable relations between each and all nations as well as participation in the United Nations organization. Without question, this is a responsibility the government must assume based on its constitution and the functions of its legislative and executive branches including activities of the state department.

12. Assuring Freedom of Speech (with Caveats): the Voice of the People Must Be Heard

Let it be said that vox populi is the sine qua non of a democratic form of government. Without it, how can our political representatives know our needs, attitudes and sentiments? Without it, how can our neighbors, near and far, know our thoughts and we theirs? In any form, oral, printed, electronic broadcast, via internet or any other means, freedom of speech, as iterated in the constitution, is the embodiment of an open society. Yet our very discourse, if not clearly defined, may lead to tragic circumstance if not curtailed at extreme limits and outright lies. By its very nature, the voice of individuals should not be misinterpreted to include the voice of money of large, wealthy domestic entities or foreign powers. Enjoy this freedom but be en-garde. This must be of concern at federal government level if only to ensure its perpetuity without restraint or dilution.

13. Promotion of Technological Research and Maintenance of Technical Standards

These days we have reached the point of necessity of scientific research as a means of survival in our overpopulated world (stem cell research, DNA evaluation, discovery of new non-fossil energy sources, communication advances, transportation improvements, environment related technologies etc.). This is so important that we can't solely rely on private enterprise to drive such needed research in directions which may not necessarily yield the fastest profit but which may discover some life saving attributes. The government, at federal and state levels, must provide an impetus in these areas so as to advance this research.

Further, it is the responsibility of the federal government to keep and maintain geo-physical and other standards such as length and distance, speed of light, time (accuracy), Global Positioning System (GSP), frequency or wavelength (and control of their use) as well as similar basic components for science and manufacturing (for interchangeability). Or would you rather see a private free-for-all in declaring who has the best standards and who shall keep them?

14. Promotion and Encouragement of the Arts

After all is said and done, what remains of a civilization as evidence of its existence despite its wars and pestilence is only its art in all forms. In a way it is manifest proof of some intelligent life on earth. The ancient Greeks had their renowned philosophers, writers, and mathematicians whose contributions to worldly understanding are well known. But then who remembers, with some exceptions, the names of their contemporary politicians and kings? Then there are the ancient Egyptians and Romans who were well versed in architecture and civil engineering as exemplified by pyramids and roads and bridges. (I don't consider warfare an art form). What a grim place this earth would be indeed without our arts, which are essentially expressions of our inner being. Ten thousand year old wall paintings have been found in caves that were eventually followed millennia later by the great European artists of the late middle ages and the renaissance to modern times. The art of the Far East in all possible forms has been on display for centuries for all to see and admire. Lately, American art has taken a well-earned seat among the great art cultures of the world including aboriginal art. Art has been with us a long time and hopefully will continue to be.

Humanity is a rather tragic species given its procliv-ity for general mayhem and even the killing of its own members for self inspired reasons or none. Its only re-deeming quality is its art which is defined here as visual, performing (including music and plays), science and engineering, architecture, literature, philosophy and ed-ucation. In essence, such activities are highly creative and beyond the realm of simple survival and gover-nance. And they should therefore be stimulated and encouraged without political influence. A nation that abandons its art creation is doomed to oblivion because art is its only true legacy. Culture bespeaks the nature of its people. Careful guidance and stimulation should not be subject to political influence and judgment.

Today a large aspect of our art appreciation is in the form of performing arts. Nearly all groups engaged in this profession exist mostly on an unsteady, insufficient, philanthropic basis. If a country is concerned with hav-ing a viable arts function it must encourage the arts of its people and consider a decent, continuous endow-ment (without imposing any political direction) to help the sustenance and continuity of a respectable arts entity representative of the essence of its people.

15. Provision of Good and Adequate Recreational Areas and Parks

The need for national parks was decided over 150 years ago in the U.S.A. during the time when home-steading and hunting were rapidly depleting available land, forests, and the animal population. John Muir was the leading early unstoppable voice here in trying to convince the federal government to preserve the beautiful natural wilderness areas of this country for the enjoyment of present and future generations. Those were the days of unlimited hunting when the bison in the great plains were nearly shot to extinction and the passenger pigeon was actually hunted to extinction; when there was no limit to private exploitation of the land by deforestation and mining; where access to wild areas for hiking and other outdoor recreation was extremely limited for the general public.

This was a white man's problem brought about by great and rapid population growth several orders of magnitude greater than that of the resident American Indians (or first nations people as the Canadians term them) at the time. The indigenous population coast-to-coast was about 300,000 while the white, mainly European, newcomers numbered in excess of 30,000,000 in the 1860's and growing. The Indians, though often fighting among themselves, always regarded the land they occupied with its trees, water, blue skies, fish and animals as holy entities not to be abused beyond their survival requirements. In effect they had been living in a giant park for thousands of years preserved by their way of life. (Refer to chapter 6, "How Can You Buy or Sell the Earth"? where Indian chief Seattle explains the Indian view of life to an American president in 1854).

After many years of political infighting the national parks came into being, a good number during President Theodore Roosevelt's administration. Today our great national parks are the pride and joy of the American people. What would this country be like without Yellowstone, Bryce, Zion, Sequoia, Yosemite, and many others? They are visited by millions every year and are run by the Parks Department within the federal government's Department of the Interior. This responsibility must remain under the jurisdiction of the federal government in perpetuity to prevent the parks from falling prey to private interests. Currently, many states have joined the federal government in providing and maintaining local parks and recreational areas to good public advantage.

16. Provision of Technical Control of Communication Media

In today's age of communication and information, I don't think anyone can seriously question the necessity for governmental authority and oversight over our communication systems which comprise commercial broadcast and cable television, satellite transmissions including the Global Positioning System, telephone and smart cell phones of all kinds, military systems, homeland security, and much else. Through the Federal Communication Commission (FCC), established in 1934 in the United States, the government allocates frequency bands and power level requirements and limitations even including radar and microwave oven radiation. The entire useable radio frequency spectrum, comprising all bands, is actually owned by the public. Certain bands and bandwidths are allocated for the various needs cited above to prevent undesirable interference of simultaneous information transmission and must be strictly adhered to. Digital data and voice packet transmission protocols and speed follow internationally agreed upon rules for telephony and satellite function. Providing security via encryption and other means is a top priority in this age of wanton cyber-terrorism and just plain hackers. Somehow, the Internet and the up-coming Facebook seem to exist today without control by any entity except perhaps by advertisers.

The FCC is required to foster competition, facilitate digital transmission, and provide access to reliable broadband products such as television particularly in its recent high definition form. At times there has been moaning and groaning about the poor content of program material produced by companies such as CBS, NBC, ABC and others for public consumption. Fifty or so years ago Newton Minow, then head of the FCC, commented in a speech to a gathering of the National Association of Broadcasters about the excessive violence and frivolity of TV programs that "when TV is good, it's best; but when bad it's the worst. Watch it for a full day and you will observe a *vast wasteland.*" With the exception of the Public Broadcasting System, much of general television programming, a captive of advertisers and immediate profits, has unfortunately deteriorated further since then.

Though TV program material can certainly stand a lot of improvement, let's keep the government's FCC operating for our lasting benefit.

17. Staying Out of Religious Affairs

With so many religions floating around the country these days, who is to say which one should be the flag bearer? Since each religion deems itself to be singularly the best and only, all others must take a back seat. It is undeniably the best course of action or inaction for the country to stay clear of religious intent and the creation of laws with religious implications which may fit one religion to the dismay of all the others plus nonreligious folk. The U.S. constitution realized this in its Amendment I which declared: "Congress shall make no law respecting an establishment of religion, or prohibiting the free exercise thereof". This is a directive not a suggestion. And a good one it is. Yet, how to explain that all denominations of our money bear the statement "In God We Trust" (all others use a credit card, I suppose)? However, sticking strictly to secular law has presented difficulties in modern times because certain religious communities have seen fit to influence some members of congress to promote legislation beneficial to them alone. Recent Supreme Court decisions have also borne the tint of religious suasion. There will always be tension between religionists and secularists regarding law; let's hope the federal constitution prevails.

18. Assuring the Best Hi-Tech and Honest Voting Procedures

The idea of people within a nation being able to vote for political leaders and representatives to guide them presupposes the existence of a democratic national government under which votes can be cast to select the desired persons. Alas, this supposition may be fractured since many autocratic leaders and their cronies have resorted to 'elections' to sustain themselves in power. So democracy has contenders, but as Winston Churchill is credited in opining, democracy may be terrible for getting things done, but all alternative forms so far devised are much worse.

Democracy, as defined in the dictionary, holds that the state should be controlled by <u>all</u> the people, each sharing equally in privileges, benefits, duties and responsibilities, each participating in the governing process.

Democracy in today's world of large overcrowded nations depends on a massed heterogeneous input as the "wisdom of the crowds". Some may praise this while others warn of a dangerous ever-growing herd mentality. Individuals, as voters, may serve as neurons with little or no comprehension of what the 'mass' brain is thinking. The wisdom may evolve inherently, naturally, depending on education and/or innate wisdom. Or it can be instilled by propaganda-like means ie., bought by ad money. Does democracy breed mediocrity which in turn may be toxic to great leadership? If democracy depends on an informed electorate, what should that information consist of? How should it be provided? What should the end result of democracy be? The most comfort and happiness for the most people? The ultimate luxury of a few at the expense of the many? The presidential election of 2000, which was ultimately settled by the Supreme Court rather than by the voting public, should give one pause in attempting to evaluate the status of American democracy.

A democratic form of representative government depends, of course, on the honest election of the people's representatives. Sounds easy to achieve but, sadly, it is not. Ideally, the voting public is well and honestly informed, the candidates intelligent and well-educated, the campaigns informative and without coercion, the voting process simple, clear, honest, reliable, well-directed and fully recorded for examination using late technology. Has this actually happened yet? Can the governing body being elected be relied upon to sustain such a voting process? Going forward, there will always be constant tension between sides, but ultimately only the national government, with its faults, can responsibly oversee the election procedure.

19. Controlling and Licensing the Use and Availability of All Non-Military Guns in the U.S.

Imagine the unlimited, unlicensed proliferation of guns and related weapons throughout the population of a country where every person owns or has access to one or more guns or equivalent dangerous weapons. Where everyone packs heat. Is this truly the key to personal safety? Could it inhibit rational conversation between individuals in favor of instant success or failure in discourse by the discharge of a gun? Would it signal a return to the age of pistol dueling? Are these weapons to be used solely for the purpose of hunting, target practice, political advancement, collecting, or self-protection? Is it legal?

For a good number of years those promoting such activity have taken refuge in the apparent safety of the somewhat loosely worded second amendment of the U.S. constitution which states: "A well regulated Militia, being necessary to the security of a free State, the right of the people to keep and bear Arms, shall not be infringed". As an amendment, it was added to the constitution following ratification some 230 years ago, an era when the predominant weapons were sabers, swords, muskets and flintlocks and powder and balls. There were then only three million colonists and perhaps 300,000 American Indians and lots of wilderness. A revolutionary war against the British had just been won and the new constitution described a new form of government with a congress and a president. As part of that document a Militia was defined as one of the protecting elements of the country.

Article I section 8 of the constitution says the Congress shall have the power "to provide for calling forth the Militia to execute the Laws of the Union, suppress Insurrections and repel Invasions"; further, that section also states that Congress shall have the power to provide for organizing, arming, and disciplining, the Militia". Article II section 2 says "the President shall be Commander in Chief ..... of the Militia of the several States when called into the actual Service of the United States". A Militia is thus defined by the constitution, prior in time to the incorporation of the second amendment, in three places as a well-trained, governmentally controlled army for specific governmental purposes rather than being a single armed individual or a group of armed individuals not responsive to governmental control.

A NICE BIG BROTHER ❯

The fathers of our country could not possibly have envisioned today's automatic weapons fed with multiple rounds of ammunition to ensure quick, deadly results. Against animals? Against neighbors? Against some inanimate target? Against fellow humans? Can anyone today sensibly justify the need for the retention of a personal armory? Perhaps for collection like stamps or artwork. Time and again in recent decades there have been assassinations by guns of major public figures, wholesale killings in public forums, schoolyards and even the schoolhouses themselves (Columbine, Virginia Tech et al.), some by children who were able to obtain guns indirectly under present laws. In recent years over 30,000 people per year have died from gun violence in the United States. But what has this got to do with 'Militias being necessary for the security of a free state' in the second amendment which proponents constantly cite as their modus vivendi?

If grammar of the English language today is still considered as viable as was used in that amendment, then as stated there, necessary Militias exist as the only reason for the people to have the right bear arms. 'A Militia being necessary for security' has the same meaning as 'because a Militia is needed for security' is a clear statement of sole purpose. Moreover, citing 'the people' as opposed to persons in the second amendment presupposes that 'the people' is to be construed as the country's population at large ready to protect itself against some onslaught. Therefore there does not appear to be a constitutionally legal right for individuals to bear arms

95 ❯

except for the purpose of performing duty for a military armed force.

Reference to the second Amendment begun by the National Rifle Association in the early seventies in the wake of the assassinations of Martin Luther King Jr. and Robert F. Kennedy to justify the carrying of a gun by anyone is way off target. No less a conservative stalwart than Judge Robert Bork said, in 1989, that the Constitution's Second Amendment guaranteed "the right of states to form Militias, not for individuals to bear arms". In 1991 former Chief Justice Warren Burger said that the NRA's interpretation of the Second Amendment was "one of the greatest pieces of fraud, I repeat the word 'fraud', on the American public by special interest groups that I have ever seen in my lifetime." That should lay to rest the connection between personal weapons and constitutional permission.

On the other hand, the constitution does not specifically prohibit anyone from bearing weapons of any kind, anywhere, for any purpose. Unrestricted, the weapons might even include, in addition to guns, cannons, hand-tossed or rocket propelled grenades, improvised explosive devices, and any of a host of other ingenious killing devices. This sort of freedom gets mighty close to the definition of terrorism for which federal laws have been enacted to provide a degree of national security. Once the public discussion devolves around types of weapons allowable, sanity of potential owners, specific areas where the weapons can be toted plus other factors, no restrictive law can ever be enacted because, having entered this losing conversation, proponents will argue, as they always have, that any small restriction will eventually lead to total prohibition.

This country is quite large and it is recognized that the protection needs of folks in vast rural or even wild places is far different from that of an urban setting patrolled by police. So if some feel they need means of self-protection which, by the way, statistically comprises only one percent of the reasons for all the gun murders in the U.S., by all means get your preferred weapon but strictly under the conditions of governmental regulation and licensing to determine qualifications for ownership and use much as for a driver's license. And please, no high-speed machine guns, large ammo clips and the like which are only needed for combat in war or by governmental agencies.

20. Assuring That All Elected Government Officials Are Chosen Through a Democratic Process by the People

One thing that reasonable people can agree on is that any viable government, to be considered 'good', must be beneficial to all the people living within its jurisdiction. That can best be assured if the people are part of its formation and can exercise control of its functions. But for that to happen on a practical basis, and since all people cannot assemble at once in one place without chaos to make a common government work properly (creating laws to live by, their enforcement and the like) for all constituents to enjoy, history tells us that representative democracy, wherein persons are chosen to represent different segments of (and cumulatively all) the population in a common governmental function, comes closest to achieving such objectives. After all, the root of the word democracy is the Greek word demos, meaning people. The bedrock of a democratic government is its laws and leadership which provide the necessary responsiveness to the needs of its people through their representatives.

Democracy, in essence, is a form of constant bickering among a large pluralistic group of people in order to attain some unclear goal of ever-changing self-governance. It must simultaneously deal with the dreams of the ignorant and the wise, the poor and the wealthy, the hale and the sick, of different ethnic and religious backgrounds in various numbers, with ambiguous legal language, willing to live together under conditions of changing and advancing technology and thought. It must do all this in an attempt to provide a common desirable basis for living together for the common good of all or most. And what seems best for one generation may not work as well or at all for the next. There is a question as to whether this is achievable. But either take that or accept arbitrary, selfish, dictatorial, most likely religion based, life-direction from a single individual or small cabal. There is much historical evidence of the failure of ancient and modern states with such regimes which have produced endless wars, extensive poverty and suffering and early death for most and benefit for the fewest. Maybe in trying to discover the best governmental or societal form, we may be overlooking the fact that the real issue is actually the diversity and inequality of human behavior which, if ever understood, will lead to a most ideal form of government. Meanwhile, the ancient Greeks may have had it right in espousing democracy. Winston Churchill said that democracy as a system is quite flawed but none better has come along.

Democracy is a social contract between individuals and their government whereby individuals agree to abide by common rules and accept corresponding duties and responsibilities to protect themselves and one another from violence and other kinds of harm and reap the benefits of an orderly, law-based society. A government's legitimacy comes from the citizens' delegation to the government of their rights of self-preservation and equality of justice for all. Government thus derives its just powers from the consent of the governed as stated in the Declaration of Independence of the United States.

Ideally, in a representative democracy, competent persons are chosen at all levels on the basis of plurality by means of an agreed to and honest voting process to address and evaluate carefully, thoughtfully and thoroughly the issues at hand for the benefit and best interests of his or her electorate with due concern for the needs of concomitant factions with whom we must share a common regime. The competence of the elected officials should be based on education, experience and knowledge of the responsibilities of his or her office plus demonstrated oratorical, managerial and leadership qualities as needed. Sounds like a dream from a far off planet but that's what is needed to effectuate a stable, caring government. It doesn't exist yet apparently and gets more difficult to achieve the larger the area and the population within its dominion.

It is sensible to examine what aspects must be considered in attempting to form a sustainable, representative government.

- Should our own representative reflect our collective ignorance and prejudices or perhaps an elitist version thereof to best enhance our favors before those of all other factions in governmental sessions regardless of our moral concerns?
- It is interesting to note that the American constitution has no qualification statement for any office, not even reading and writing, except age (25 years for representatives, 30 for senators, 35 for president): should it?
- Should our representative be chosen on the basis of competence, or wealth, or political or religious suasion, or figurative vision, or gender, or straight or gay attitude, all the above, or other?
- Is such a process established by a constitution?
- Can a single government entity satisfy widely divergent needs of various cohorts of people living in a large area (such as the United States) with diverse resources such as water, ores, land fertility and cultivability, wet or dry and cold or warm

weather, mountains and valleys, dense or scarce population, heavy or light industrial regions, rural and urban areas?

- Are the powers of office well defined with pro-scribed limits to those powers?
- Is the process of election clearly understood i.e., should representatives be chosen on the basis of plurality of voters or other method, neither stated nor implied in the constitution?
- Is there a reasonable process for removal from office of representatives for malfeasance?
- Has malfeasance in office been clearly defined in any official document?
- Is the latest validated technology being used to ensure honest elections?
- Should voting be voluntary?
- Should there be a minimum intelligence level for voters as well as representatives?
- How many persons should each representative serve? The U.S. constitution says there shall be at most one rep per 30,000 colonists with a total of 65 declared at the outset when the constitution was ratified. At that rate the total today would be in the order of 10,000 representatives if the same limit applied. At present, each representative serves 600,000 constituents.
- What is the best way to engage in and pay for campaigns for public office?
- Are there moral responsibilities which should be adhered to in public office?

- Under representative democracy can we get the best possible leadership or must we settle for the most popular which may be mediocre? And if not why not?

Should these questions ever be answered, new ones are bound to pop up ad infinitum. Governmental democracy is mankind's most precious gift but it is an ever evolving process. And that's as it ought to be. I think the ancient Greeks were right in believing that nothing endures except change.

21. Establishing and Empowering a National Bill of Rights for all Citizens

The enumeration and descriptions of good government in the preceding sections is, in a sense, a roster of common legal restraints and license needed to allow people to live together in safety, peace, economic security, comfort, and generally without personal harm. Its necessity and scope seem to grow in proportion to the numbers living under its aegis. Yet there is an important aspect that must be included as part of good government and that is a constitutionally established bill of rights and freedoms that is applicable equally for rich and poor alike, in all areas of the country, in perpetuity, including common law assuring equal legal protection. You'd think that creating such a document would be a pushover since its chief beneficiary is the public who presumably demand it and then elect the very officials who would create, enact and indeed empower it. Alas, that is not the case: so far in the United States it has taken over two centuries to frame it in the form of constitutional rights and amendments. It is still a work in progress.

These rights and freedoms are not to be construed as behavioral restrictions for the populace but as equal guarantees for the benefit of all. It is the responsibility of those living within its benevolence to make these rights and freedoms come alive by assuring, through action and constitutional amendments, that there be no discrimination in any activity of the government at any level with regard to gender, race or color, ethnic origin, religion, or sexual orientation. Further, our way of life should embody tolerance of differences between people, privacy, the ability for the public to address grievances legally, personal security, the freedoms of speech, worship, from want, from fear and economic insecurity. Mix all these together and we can go forward with the promise of a good, happy life.

22. Adherence to a Constitution and Law

All the forgoing is of no avail if the people do not abide by a publicly chosen and agreed upon constitution and accompanying laws. This is a major consideration when one realizes that the only alternatives are dictatorial regimes headed by tyrants or monarchs along with their accompanying enforcers or barring that, general anarchy. If private property is considered the root of freedom then personally defending it from robbery or incursion becomes a necessity for survival under the condition of anarchy which has no rules except that established by individual weapon size and effectiveness.

That kind of 'rugged individualism' of the past might suffice to protect one from a half-dozen or so felons but against modern criminal gangs, illegal computer-hacking, and numerous neighbors with possible evil intent would be obviously hopeless. An agreed upon government based on law seems best if it isn't created by a single well-thinking individual. Abraham Lincoln said that a government is needed to do for the people what they as individuals cannot do by themselves and <u>no more</u>. That is a thoughtful, wise, observation that works as long as the powers of government are not diluted to the point of ineffectiveness as has been proposed at times by various political groups in the U.S. And, of course, the government must be endowed by law with the ability to monitor and enforce its constitutional prerogatives.

23. Creating and Maintaining a National Budget

When people choose to live together as citizens of a common nation they embark on a journey of mutual reliance and advantage as well as of shared sacrifice which must be borne and paid for in the real world by establishing a monetary budget. This can never be a static affair since population growth and its distribution, evolving transportation and communication needs, reconsideration of priorities, variations in natural environment, and a host of other factors will always combine to demand frequent budgetary review.

If we agree on the 22 preceding elements of a good government then, of necessity, the cost of ensuring their implementation, even if only modestly at the outset, has to be considered. Needless to say, good sense demands that reserve funds be created to address and pay for unpredictable and unforeseen future events such as earthquakes, storms, floods, forest fires, sudden unavailability of fossil fuels, power grid failures, conflicts, attacks and the like over some limited time period. Deriving an acceptable budget depends on the nation's GDP and the ability of its citizens to understand that, barring triage, we're all responsible for each of us and therefore an estimated 15% to 20% of our budget must always be devoted to caring for the disabled and less fortunate among us without the constant bickering over that line item's necessity or continual dependence on religious institutions and philanthropy to fulfill that need.

A government that is established to fulfill a mission of governance and provide the social needs of its citizens that they themselves or their private enterprises cannot satisfactorily provide must get sufficient funds by some means of progressive taxation from its citizens and their organizations in order to properly function at the national, state and local levels. Expect that there will always be tension between expenditure priorities and funding sources thus assuring continued employment for congressional members and their staffs.

Finally….

No doubt, after reading A Nice Big Brother, some may moan and groan and feel a sense of overkill in my defining a government whose responsibilities seem to plunge further into our personal lives than they think necessary. After all, the 230 year-old U.S. constitution, comprising only a handful of pages including the amendments, has served us well over the years.

That constitution provides basically a terse description of a *form* of government which can collect taxes, pay debts, coin money, establish and maintain an army and a navy, establish a post office, declare war, regulate commerce, borrow money and promote science and the arts. That's it. It does not offer or direct *how* or *what* things to do for the country's successful survival over the centuries going forward from the present.

Life today is much different and more complex from that of the days when the constitution was created by the thoughtful men who wore tricorn hats. Those were days when medical attention was derived from a barber pole, transportation over land was by horse in any form, education was private and minimally required, fuel and heating were obtained by burning tree wood, electricity or a power grid didn't exist and wasn't even planned yet, military sophistication was a musket with ball and powder, communication was face-to-face or on paper, industrialization hadn't occurred yet, international relations was an emerging art form as was banking.

The population now is over 100 times greater than it was in 1780 and in many places people are living cheek to jowl in multi-storied apartment buildings and getting to hi-tech jobs via public transportation in sophisticated vehicles or trains or private cars. Or getting to far flung places quickly by airliners. A vast electrical power grid is in place and growing to provide the energy needed to sustain this modern civilization. Further, two young college graduates getting married now may start out with a combined college mortgage almost equivalent to the mortgage of a new home. Life, being more complex, a much higher level of education is mandatory than in the past for a person to be effective in today's workforce.

It makes little sense to base our present and future ways of life and ideas on a centuries' old document with "strict interpretation thereof" rules without updating and clarifying its intent. The objective of A Nice Big Brother is to indicate important areas to which government responsibilities should now be clearly extended to accommodate modern and near term foreseeable activities of a growing nation and to suggest, in effect, a number of amendments to accomplish that. Why amendments instead of laws? Because as has been so evident over many years, laws may be enacted and just as quickly deactivated by the courts and legislature as the nation falls prey to the politics of the day. This approach, which we currently witness, creates uncertainty and instability in the daily lives of people. Amendments are more difficult to enact and destroy thereby inducing a greater degree of thought in their formulation. (Amendments 18 and 21 dealing with the enactment and repeal of Prohibition in 1919 and 1933 respectively are exceptions.)

The suggestions of A Nice Big Brother do not change one iota of the original constitution's intent or text, they simply modernize it and add details to the rules of governance that modern life demands to proceed adequately into the future.

What one learns from all this is that as more and more people share this planet more rules and technology are needed to enable us to live together in comfort and safety.

CHAPTER **11**

Pilgrims' Progress

LIFE IS CHANGE. You go from young to old to gone: birth to earth. So far I've seen two generations pass into the dustbin of history. The people currently inhabiting the planet are, for the most part, a new and different cohort than before with entirely new experiences and attitudes. One expects that. What I point out here are some of the key changes in lifestyle brought about by technological, political, and social forces that I have observed during the past half century or so since I became aware of things outside myself. As with earlier generations, young people today (2000+) have little appreciation of the new artifacts and ideas they are flooded with daily; these are accepted as a normal environment. But those of a certain age are constantly reminded that they were born before:

- television, polio shots, frozen foods, Xerox, contact lenses, frisbees, jet flight, solar panels, power lawn mowers, hip and knee replacements, and air pollution.

- radar, credit cards, atom bombs, laser beams and ball-point pens; pantyhose, electric blankets, drip-dry clothes, computers, space travel and walking on the moon.

- house-husbands, gay rights, computer dating, dual careers, day care centers, group therapy and nursing homes, artificial hearts, yogurt, and guys wearing earrings.

- sex changes, condominiums, rock music, MacDonalds, designer jeans, AIDS, the internet, chat rooms, cell phones, fiber optics, and satellite communication.

- spin doctors, floppy and compact discs, the EPA, heart bypass operations, DVDs, water fluorida-tion, electronic hearing aids, microwave ovens, e-mail, and Walkmans.

- stick-on postage stamps, CDs, VCRs, digital time-pieces, same sex marriages, audio and video tapes, cell phones, I-pads, DNA and cloning; the list goes on.

That's more change in a generation or so than ever be-fore in the history of man. Is there any wonder there's a generation gap now?

In the days of yore, GRASS was mowed, COKE was a cold drink, and POT was something you cooked in; a JOINT was an elbow, a CHIP was a piece of wood, hard-ware meant hardware, and software wasn't even a word.

We got married first and lived together...... How quaint can you get? And we were probably the last generation that was so dumb as to think you needed a wife or husband to have a baby!

No wonder we are so confused and there is such a generation gap.

Yet somehow we are survivors.

.....And coming in the near term.......
- Completion of genetic sequencing technology
- The realization of the need for population containment down to a sustainable, comfortable level
- Fully electric vehicles
- Attainment of high energy, non-fossil power sources
- World-wide availability of all the world's information
- Development of consistent sustainable food production, with high purity and safety and low-cost distribution
- Cheap water desalinization
- Advancement leaps in computer capability and the web/internet in much smaller size
- Development of a stable world-wide banking system coupled with a "hybridist" economic system
- Total illumination by LEDs (light emitting diodes)
- Learning more thoroughly how nature works

.....And in the far term.....
- World-wide individual identification via stored genetic and medical information on a small portable plastic card or embedded chip

- 3-dimensional television
- Virtual disappearance of books in favor of electronic information presentation
- Total biodegradable packaging so there will be no need for garbage pickup or landfill sites for waste
- Total skeletal and body part regeneration or replacement
- Human sensor (seeing and hearing) replacement by non-organic components
- Brain modification to reduce or eliminate crime or mental illness
- Ability to provide sustained drug feed for a year or more without capsules or tablets
- Mind or matter teleportation to eliminate airports, airplanes, trains and traffic congestion
- The political force against public benefit will fade and we will live in peace.

CHAPTER 12

Terror in Our Time

IT'S A SAFE bet that Steven Spielberg thought he was creating the ultimate scary, hi-tech horror flicks with his
Jurassic Park dinosaur series not to mention his depic-
tion of the Holocaust and World War II horrors close up
in Schindler's List and Saving Private Ryan: protrayals of
the depths of human madness gone awry. Who could
imagine anything more frightful? But they were historic
or in a sense once-removed from our daily consciousness. If Spielberg was looking for a truly frightening
subject on which to base his films he totally overlooked
and could never have envisioned that the subject for the
most terrifying film possible was and is a scourge lurk-
ing all around him and us here and now which today
threatens the survival of humanity over the entire globe.
Overlooked, that is, until the occurrence of the terrifying
atrocities of September 11, 2001.

Could that scourge, as it has evolved in modern
times, be Islam?

Islam, the seemingly peaceful religion of history with its stories of the Arabian nights? The mathematicians and librarians of earlier cultures, at a time when nearly all of Europe was caught up in its own religious nightmare? Or today's Islam of fundamentalism, fanaticism, and with hatred of Western culture and Jews so deep as to prompt the murder of thousands of innocent people 7000 miles from its birthplace in Mecca/Medina, Saudi Arabia? Can there ever be a logical or religious explanation of reasons for such evil? Had Spielberg tackled that subject and created a truthful movie about it, the Islamists would have no doubt put a fatwa (murder contract) out on him as they have on Salman Rushdie and numerous others. Some fatwas have been actually carried out. They are not trivial: over 15,000 of them were issued by the Ayatollah Khomeini alone! More to the point, although without official religious authority in the Islamic world, Osama Bin Laden, the late leader of the al-Qaeda terrorist organization, issued a fatwa in 1998 against the United States. We weren't listening. In 1993 Muslims bombed the World Trade Center in New York City. That was an explicit warning; we paid no heed.

Founded as it was on the bloody conquest of southern Asia, the Middle East, northern Africa, and substantial portions of southern Europe starting about 1300 years ago, Islam today exhibits no tolerance for any other religious presence or belief or even some variations in Islamic belief. (Sunnis, Wahabbis, Shi'ites, Baathists and Hashemites have fought and killed each other for centuries.) Conflicts in the Middle East and the Indian sub-continent as well as in Indonesia, Malaysia, and the Philippines bear this out. Israel, a tiny splinter of a state seemingly lost in the millions of empty square miles of Islamic desert, causes intolerable indigestion to Muslims: they can't abide the Jews there nor any entity that supports their presence. Astoundingly, the Arabs maintain to this day that the Israelis are bent on attacking Arabia to reclaim Medina because some Jews lived there thousands of years ago before and during the time of Muhammed!

This intolerance is based, for the most part, on the explicit instructions given to its adherents in the Qu'ran, the effective Islamic equivalent of the Christian bible. According to one of its main tenets, those not following "the true path of Allah", "those who have incurred Your (Allah's) wrath and have gone astray" are considered infidels and must be caused to perish. Bernard Lewis, a leading expert on Middle East culture, states in his book The Middle East that "classical Islamic law is based frankly on inequality, since it would be inappropriate and indeed absurd to accord equal treatment to those who accept God's final revelation and those who willfully reject it". Islam's rejection of infidels, Christians and especially Jews, is not unlike the rejection (excommunication) of heretics and Jews by the European church for more than a thousand years. Is this aspect of rejection a sine qua non of organized religion? In all fairness it must be said that nearly all religions have gone through a maturation phase of intense proselytizing, conversion, massacres and inquisitions, self purification, with eventual reformation, self-reflection and examination, reevaluation and final emergence as a viable source of moral guidance.

With Islam, a relatively late religion, the worst upheavals just happen to be occurring in our time and, without external intervention, will continue to occur in the near and even foreseeable future. Muslim fanaticism long predates the West's global influence. It can be argued that it was precisely such fanaticism that caused the backwardness of much of the Muslim world. As with followers of other faiths, all Muslims are not cookie-cutter clones, they cover the gamut of mild adherents to extremist fanatics. As we now know, the discernment of the latter is a life or death proposition. Keen observation tells us that Islam's intolerance seems to diminish somewhat with distance from its epicenter, Arabia. That may partially explain why the Jews, while being cursed and killed throughout Europe during the Middle Ages, flourished for hundreds of years in remote Islamic Spain (until the Inquisition).

Buried within the 114 chapters and many suras (comprising the shari'a—instructions for living) of the Qu'ran is the concept of "inshallah" which means simply: if God (Allah) wanted certain things to happen or not he would have done so. If He did not create or instruct it, you as a Muslim are enjoined from so doing, such as developing new ideas and making secular progress in science, economics, medicine, agriculture, law, and the like. That's just what's been happening to this day and explains why many young Muslims travel to Europe and the United States to get an education. But they face an intractable problem when they return home: what to do with their newly acquired education, with its Qu'ranic conflicts, in their homeland where there is usually severe unemployment. Those Muslims exposed to Western culture (sleazy though it may be at times) become envious, frustrated and even resentful beyond measure at the realization that following their own path of no progress leads to a dead end. Islam is a relatively young religion but frozen in time at its creation around the year 700 seemingly without the possibility of adaptive change to the vicissitudes of life style say, by "constitutional amendment" or "reformation", perhaps, leaving only interpretation as a way around its strict shari'a. Can a religion rooted in the belief that all truth was revealed to its prophet, Muhammed, and none since then ever successfully embrace change?

According to Bernard Lewis, the nearest Muslim approach to the Christian concept of heresy is embodied in the term "bid'a" meaning innovation. Observance of tradition is good; departure from tradition is bid'a: heretical. The traditionalist view is well summed up in a saying attributed to the Prophet: "the worst things are those that are novelties. Every novelty is an innovation, every innovation is an error and every error leads to hellfire". Therefore, change is an anathema to be avoided, while respect and belief for the tradition, finality and perfection of the Muslim revelation are to be followed. Bid'a is a transgression. Thus the Qu'ran has so far succeeded in hermetically sealing off the possibility of new thought from the believers of Islam. Progress toward peace and understanding between Islam and the rest of the world will come only when Islamic leaders figure a safe way out of this impasse.

This religious intransigence and rejection of new ideas, secular thought and technical innovation creates a poverty, that on the present scale, provides the breeding ground for international pathologies: support for terrorism, narco-trafficking, massive migration flows, and thereby the spread of infectious diseases and thought.

The treatment of women under fundamentalist orthodox Islam is an absolute abomination beyond normal reason. Regarded as chattel, not allowed and education, with essentially no legal status or protection, covered from head to toe in public or otherwise beset by public beatings or having acid thrown in the face for the least infraction by patrolling religious police, especially in Saudi Arabia (and the Taliban regions of Afghanistan before the recent war), this denigration of the female half of Islam is truly a recipe for cultural disaster. How can this be considered a sensible way of life?

Worse, these conditions are institutionalized and self perpetuated from generation to generation: figurative inoculation at birth, indoctrination (brain washing) in childhood, plus lifelong propaganda from state or religious institutions. Each succeeding graduating class provides an endless stream of new terrorists to train the next and so on indefinitely. Terror is also promulgated by the payment of large sums of money ($10,000 to $15,000) by various Islamic countries and organizations to the families of "martyrs" (shahidi) who die in the service of Islam. Under these circumstances how can terrorism ever end of its own accord?

Many Muslims, especially among the 7 million living in the U.S., say they reject fundamentalist Islamic teaching and its derived terrorism. They pray and provide substantial charitable donations to their mosques, fully realizing that a substantial portion of that money goes to support numerous terrorist organizations including Hamas, Hisballah, Islamic Jihad and Al Qaeda. Although claiming not to be ostensibly active in, sympathetic to, or acceptive of terrorist activities, I have so far not read or heard one word uttered by any Muslim anywhere stating directly that he or she fully condemns terrorism and particularly the atrocities of September 11, perpetrated by Muslims, when over 3000 innocent people, including airline passengers and crew were killed at the World Trade Center, the Pentagon, and in a field in Pennsylvania. To kill even one person in the name of God is blasphemy; to massacre thousands of innocent men, women, and children is an obscene perversion of religion. Yet invariably, their words of sorrow about these events are quickly accompanied by statements of resentment about the misbehavior of Western powers and of past American foreign policy indiscretions, particularly its support for Jews and Israel, that cry out for retribution. Is this apparent lack of contrition caused by fear of retribution by their fellow worshippers? Despite the reasons that caused them to migrate here, it appears they are generally very loyal to Islam, praying 5 times a day.

An examination of the modern map of the "greater" middle east, the Islamic Heartland below, shows a cluster of Islamic nations from Pakistan on the east to Libya on the west (with an extended "tail", the Maghreb, along north Africa through Tunisia, Algeria, and Morocco), and from Sudan on the south to Chechnya and Kazakhstan to the north. Note that all these countries are contiguous to one another with the epicenter of this cluster being Saudi Arabia, Islam's birthplace. Unfortunately, the existence of a number of these nations and their borders were dictated at the time of European colonialism. Though

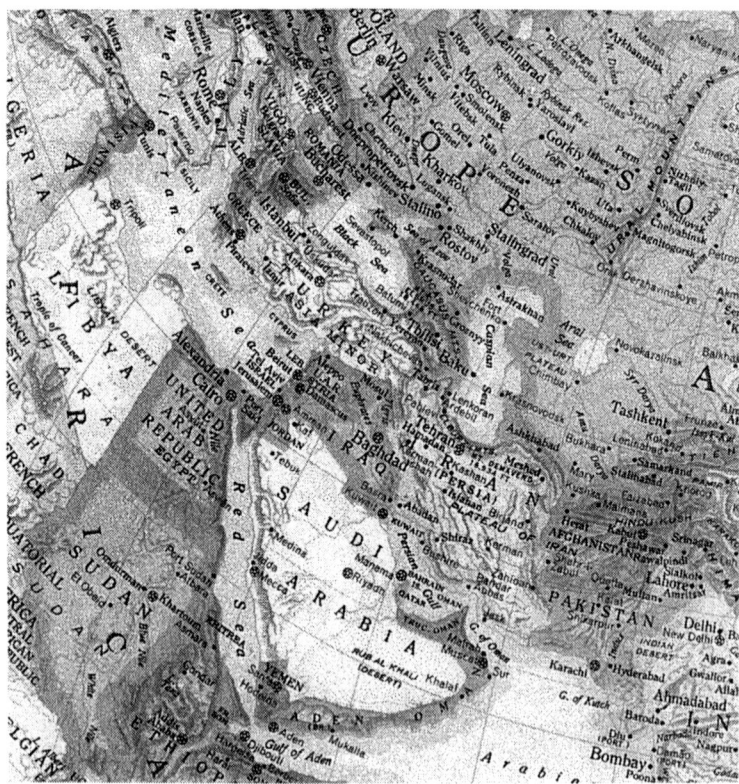

Islam does not recognize the concept of nationhood nor any national borders (except, of course, at the United Nations where their profusion as nations gives them a powerful voting bloc), most of these entities are under control of a despotic regime led by a dictator, royal family or war lords each guarding their turf from inroads or threats to their personal interpretation of religious purity. Democracy, civil liberties, and personal freedoms seem to be unknown concepts in the Muslim world. Hence the presence of the democracy of Israel in its midst is so abhorrent to Islamic sensibilities. Note that Islam makes little or no distinction between Christians and Jews; they are viewed collectively as people of the cross and hence infidels. Turkey, sharing some European soil and closely exposed to European influence and despite all its internal difficulties, is today a struggling democracy and thus may be considered an exception to the rule. However, bear in mind that just prior to its incarnation as a modern nation it was the heart of the Ottoman Empire.

The ability of these entities to support terrorism in Israel and elsewhere, including the U.S., tends to diffuse the generally intense hatred among and within themselves (Iran – Iraq, Jordan – Syria, and various tribal conflicts) while providing a sort of redirected energy outlet to keep the Islamic peoples quiescent. Couple that with ignorance, unemployment, propaganda, censorship and the Qu'ranic base to tie it all together and you have a mean brew indeed.

There has been considerable intellectual ferment in the Muslim world during the last century. Courageous and outspoken scholars and reformers have risked and lost their lives for independent writings on Islamic matters. They have been assassinated or threatened with assassination in Afghanistan, Algeria, Iran, Kuwait, Lebanon, Pakistan, Syria, Turkey, Yemen and the Western Diaspora, including the United States. There are few, if any, safe havens. Many members of the Muslim worlds' intellectual elite now live in North America and Western Europe. But the enlightenment espoused in their books cannot reach the minds of people in Muslim lands because the rate of illiteracy there is 70 to 80 percent even without the ever-present censorship.

An intractable problem the West faces in dealing with Muslim leaderships is their endemic inability to negotiate differences to arrive at agreements. Muslims come to the table armed with ultimatums. The concept of negotiation, apparently foreign to their thinking, means that opposing sides come to a table with best offers fully realizing at the outset that following negotiation each side will walk away with something less than hoped for but with an outcome both sides can agree to, with a plan to honor that agreement by signature and act, and thenceforth live in peace. Unfortunately, Muslim disagreements among themselves and with the West are only settled by force, assassination and terror rather than negotiation. A good example of this is the Israeli-Palestinian stalemate. When Ehud Barak made an offer to Yasser Arafat at a meeting at Camp David in the U.S. a few years ago, rightly or wrongly the most generous to date, Arafat totally rejected the offer and, true to Muslim tradition, never made a counter offer to Barak as one would normally expect at a negotiation. Arafat would accept only total capitulation to his needs with no bargaining. So the intifada continues. The Oslo "agreement" was simply the Palestinians stating their case as an ultimatum and waiting for Israel to give as much as it dared: "land for peace". The Palestinians gave nothing, not even peace, never made a counter offer, or even considered coming away from Oslo with anything less than their full demands. The concept of "land for peace" turned out to be a farce: years ago Arafat, when interviewed by the press declared, in response to a query about what land Israel had to give for him to be satisfied, "we Palestinians are not interested in borders".

Islam really doesn't have a viable economic system capable of sustaining its followers in reasonable comfort. To make matters worse, the Islamic Heartland is located, for the most part, in harsh, droughty desert regions and families are encouraged to have numerous children – perhaps as many as ten – which assures the perpetuation of poverty, malnutrition and illiteracy. But Allah has given Islam a heavenly blessing or so it seems. Saudi Arabia is perched on top of a vast sea of oil and there are additionally many large underground lakes of the liquid gold scattered about the region adjacent to or near Saudi Arabia. This has proven to be an immense source of wealth for the area created and shamefully sustained largely by the United States and, to a lesser extent, by Europe and others. We have poured billions upon billions of dollars into Saudi Arabia, the Croesus of

Islam, for its oil only to see the money hoarded mainly by a single family rather than being distributed to those most in need. Because of its immense oil wealth, Saudi Arabia (and not far behind, Iraq and Iran) supports every Islamic terrorist organization in the world with endless funding. As the events of 9/11 made clear, Saudi Arabia exports more than oil. We created the wherewithal to pay for the very terrorism that attacked the U.S. and are continuing to do so with every purchase of Middle-East oil. We are so beholden to that oil, that every aspect of our foreign and domestic policy is driven by it. By the same token, the Arabs are totally beholden to us for the money to sustain themselves since they have no other major viable economic resource. It is time to change the Middle East equation.

And it is time to realize we have two worlds in collision on the same planet.

To deal with Islamic terrorism, there are a number of issues that must be addressed by the United States and the Western Powers, the first of which is to realize the extent of the problem.

What is the ultimate objective of fundamentalist Islam today? Is it to convert the entire global population to Islamism? That seems most unlikely as a near-term goal. Yet Muslim jihad (holy war or struggle) is perceived by Muslims as a religious obligation that would continue until all the world has adopted the Muslim faith or submitted to Muslim rule. The Qu'ran says it is lawful to wage war against infidels and apostates. Should we wait until Islam's objectives become crystal clear in its deadliness before responding? Could it be that the total objective of al-Qaeda, currently Islam's most vicious wing, is simply to reestablish Islamic fundamentalism widely, get rid of Israel, hurt its supporters, and extirpate all Western influence from the Islamic Heartland? From the world? That's what they're telling us daily if we pay attention. To achieve that goal, al-Qaeda has metamorphosed into a self-perpetuating terror organization whose growth, like a viral disease, spreads exponentially with no limit in sight. Today it is world-wide in scope and threat.

Another issue is to determine what actions, if any, should be taken to thwart this organization and others like it. One option is to do nothing: blame ourselves for prompting terror, accept terrorism like the weather and hope we personally can survive. Be prepared to convert. The assumption that if we take action against terrorists they will react by doing something worse runs up against the probability that they are already planning to do something worse.

A second, more realistic, option is to thwart Islamic terrorism as rapidly as possible, certainly at a rate faster than its growth to be effective. To conquer such a Hydra requires simultaneous, immediate, multi-faceted, global attacks on terror. Here's a way to do it:

- Establish a global group of allied nations opposed to Islamic terrorism willing to provide adequate military, intelligence and banking assistance for the long haul.

- Develop a compatible national and global security system to share intelligence about terrorist cell activities and provide a world-wide system and network for identification of all persons by using the latest technology including DNA, magnetic-strip ID cards, encryption, eye-print, etc. to be used everywhere, especially for travel.
- Reduce our reliance on middle-east oil as rapidly as possible. Increasing vehicle efficiency by just a few miles per gallon of gasoline now would get us out of the addiction quickly and fortunately the basic technology exists to do so. Alternate fuels and energy sources that we have studied and experimented with for years should be fully developed and marketed without delay. However, for reasons of world economic stability our phase-out from the middle-east oil market must be done at a gradual pace that we establish and control rather than OPEC. Just the realization of our intention by Saudi Arabia should sit them bolt upright and perhaps curtail somewhat their support of terrorism.
- Identify and interdict the transfer of terrorist-bound funds world-wide, even from mosques in the U.S., with the cooperation of allied countries and their banking systems. This money could be used to help defray the cost of fighting terrorism.
- Release overwhelming military attacks against known terrorist groups and their bases. At present, the United States must take the lead in developing

the tactical and strategic military means to plan, coordinate and fight the terrorists on our terms anywhere. Success of this activity will take years with constant vigil thereafter.

- Set up an international judicial system to deal harshly, but humanely(?) with perpetuators of terrorism wherever they may be found. It cannot be expected that every captured terrorist can be extradited to the United States nor face American military tribunals.

- Accept no new Muslim immigrants until terror perpetuated by the Islamic world has been removed, attenuated or somehow exorcised from the world. This may take years and require the passage of special laws in this regard by congress.

- Develop a long term educational counteroffensive to combat and neutralize the incessant terrorist indoctrination (i.e. in madrasas) and propaganda generated by the Islamic religious leaders and the press.

- Announce to the Islamic world that terrorism against the West is unacceptable in any form. Any activities undertaken by them to inflict harm to other peoples of the world will be dealt with immediately and severely.

The western world must understand the realities of the dangerous world we live in and shape its policies to prevent recurrence of the September disasters or far worse. It is up to us to prove that the military actions already begun are not a prelude to another futile struggle and that our fine resolve to finish with terrorism is not just another eruption of hot air, to be followed, after a great deal of bloodshed, by yet more capitulations.

It should be realized that the above near term responses to terrorism are simply to allow life as we know it to continue with approximate normality. Any attempt by the Western powers to disestablish Islam by arms on a world-wide basis is both futile and Quixotic as is the reverse by Muslims. For the long term Islam must somehow learn to deal with modernization and Western culture. Ultimately, any lasting termination of terror must come from Islam itself with perhaps some goading by the West. It will take brilliant minds on both sides to find a way to do that by adding to or reinterpreting the total truth revealed to Mohammed by Allah many centuries ago. Only then can the world face a future of peace and enlightenment. And, of course, we should be quite wary that our own smugness does not shield us from continual self-examination and vigilance in the constant pursuit of tolerance, understanding and openness.

CHAPTER **13**

The Muddle East

If you can't describe the problem you will never find the solution.

– L.S.

WHENEVER THE U.S. administration considers the latest rampant chaos in the Israeli-Palestinian area, particularly the rash of Palestinian suicide bombings and rocket attacks, its actions in that regard seem to indicate total ignorance or total directed avoidance of understanding of the fact that there are external political, religious, and economic interests guiding the activities in that area. We talked to Ariel Sharon (then Ehud Olmert, now Bibi Netanyahu) and now, since Yasser Arafat's death in 2004, Abu Mazen/Mahmoud Abbas (who was Arafat's right-hand man for 30 years) on an equal footing, apparently making no distinction in their sense of morality and justice and as if each had equivalent control of their respective peoples. But that is not the case.

Whereas Natanyahu may be guided by internal Israeli pressure and somewhat by American politics, Abbas is guided by al Fatah, Hamas, Hesballah, Islamic Jihad, and a rich assortment of other terrorist groups such as the al Aqsa Brigade, all seeking to annihilate Israel. It is well known and published and broadcast in numerous media that the actions of these groups and Abbas are in turn well funded and directed by Saudi Arabia, Iran, Syria, Jordan, Qatar, Egypt and others. Also, every mosque in the world, including those in the U.S., sends money to the terrorists to support and continue their suicidal attacks against the Jews. In the interest of Middle East peace the U.S. should at least do its part to intercept those funds before they reach their intended recipients.

On that basis, the real key to peace there would seem to be to talk forcefully to Saudi Arabia, the wealthiest funder of all, and tell it to desist from supporting terrorism or there will be unhappy consequences. Our reliance on Saudi oil has so far inhibited our ability (maybe even our desire) to discuss that topic with the Saudis and the other Muslim nations in the area. And that, dear reader, is precisely the prima facie reason we don't have peace in the Middle East. Could it be that the U.S., by its unquenchable thirst for that region's oil, is unwittingly fueling the growth of terrorism there? Unquestionably.

But is there a deeper underlying factor which the West is somehow overlooking in trying to bring the conflicted parties to the negotiating table to at least seriously consider the current U.S. "roadmap"-to-peace plan? The answer is yes. It is clearly stated in the teachings of the Qu'ran.

Can peace ever exist there or anywhere indeed where the Qu'ran is held as an intolerant and impenetrable bulwark against Western secular law and culture? A sort of matter versus anti-matter. Islam, as espoused in its holy book the Qu'ran, is not a peaceful religion despite protestations to the contrary by most Muslims and cannot be considered an innocent bystander in today's terrorism. The words negotiation and compromise may not even exist in the Arabic language. The Qu'ran renders the concept of installing democracy as we know it anywhere in Islamic territory an absolute oxymoron. It simply will never happen.

Recall that the entire area from Morocco to Pakistan, with its many indigenous ethnic and religious peoples, including Jews, was conquered by the Arabs following the new religion of Islam 1300 years ago. Eventually, Islamic control extended to include Indonesia plus other parts of the far east region of Asia. This religion is deemed by its followers to be an updated replacement of the older, and in their view, cruder, Judeo-Christian religion. Their epicenter was and is Mecca in Saudi Arabia. As the Arab/Muslims see it, any people not of their Islamic faith are considered infidels and those infidels, like the Jews of Israel in particular, who happen to occupy a tiny speck of land surrounded essentially on three sides by hostile Muslim desert, must be annihilated. Why? Is Arab frustration with and hate of the Israeli presence so great that there is no room for cohabitation and tolerance but infinite capacity for terrorism and murder? Does Israel sit atop a vast lake of oil coveted by the Arabs? Is its meager amount of land so fertile and fruitful that it must be forfeit? Is it that those few acres of land partitioned off to the Jews as a homeland by the United Nations in 1947 following the Holocaust was seen by the Arabs as a dastardly act by infidels and, hence, must be utterly destroyed? It nearly was.

The modern history of the formation of Israel as a state and its struggle to exist is well worth reviewing as a clear example of human deviousness, intolerance, the cost of ignorance, the dreams of people, the training of hatred, religious attitudes, the dumbness of foreign governments and their associated policies which fail to grasp the immorality and horror of terrorism, and the apparent total inability of the Arabs to accept persons of another culture to live beside them. Whatever happened to the concept of human kindness? Where is their menschlichkeit anywhere?

Fundamentally, one must at least challenge the concept of a separate indigenous people called 'Palestinians' foisted by the drumbeat of incessant worldwide propaganda. They are the same Arabs that live in Syria, Jordan and Lebanon. There was never an indigenous "Palestinian" government, constitution, money, postage stamps, or even a leader. Over the centuries the area was overrun by Romans, Mamluks, Ottomans, and eventually the British who delineated and named the various nations in the vicinity. The British in November 1917 issued the Balfour Declaration (by Arthur Balfour, British Foreign Secretary) expressing approval of a Jewish homeland in the Palestine area under British control. It stated: *His Majesty's Government views with favor the establishment in Palestine of a national home for the Jewish people and will use their best endeavors to facilitate the achievement of that object.* Following World War I Great Britain received a mandate for Palestine from the League of Nations in July 1922. Sir Herbert Samuel, a British Jew, was made governor, and active encouragement of Jewish immigration was begun.

History says there was a small residual, indigenous enclave of Jews with their holy sites (including the Wailing Wall and temple remains) in Palestine for many centuries well before Islam until some Zionist European Jews, discouraged by the persistant anti-Semitic hatred they faced, started significant migration to Palestine in the late 19th century (no doubt encouraged by the publication of *The Jewish State* by Dr. Theodor Herzl in 1896). These "pioneers" were funded by a number of wealthy Jews so they could purchase land from whoever owned it and was willing to sell. There were apparently many sellers, probably some with questionable ownership including many absentee landlords. And so, after a few decades, there were many discontiguous but substantial areas and growing (depending on where the available land was) of Jewish "latecomers". But the land they could buy was a rocky desert that had to be coaxed very diligently and irrigated to yield anything edible.

In 1922 the census estimated that there were some 85,000 Jews and some 650,000 Arabs living in Palestine. As a result of the Balfour Declaration, the Jewish population increased to some 250,000 by 1935. During World War II the influx was even heavier, until Arab resistance caused cessations from time to time.

Naturally, over the years there were constant chafing and violent clashes between the Jews and their Arab neighbors, a number of whom were nomadic Bedouins. After all, the Jews, by growing crops where none had existed before, were violating *inshallah,* the Qu'ranic stricture which says, in effect, if Allah wanted that ground to yield food for humans he would have done so. Jewish immigrants contributed to a renaissance in Palestine because of the technical skills they brought into the country and the flood of financial aid from various Jewish organizations throughout the world. Arab sheiks quickly realized that the Jews, by their activities, were undermining the credibility of the teachings of the Qu'ran. And so the battle was joined. Progress versus anti-progress and frustration.

By the start of World War II, Jews in Europe, who had already lost their citizenship, businesses, synagogues, sense of dignity and self-respect as humans, were faced with the specter of imminent slaughter by the Nazi regime in its rampage throughout Europe. Many tried valiantly with limited success to escape to distant lands around the world including the United States and even Shanghai, China. Incredibly, the United States allowed only minimal entry to the desperate Jews (anti-semitism

THE MUDDLE EAST ⋎

in the U.S. was in full flower then). Most were forced to return to face their death in concentration camps along with those who never left. This was Hitler's final solution. Six million Jews were exterminated over a period of four years. What utter horror! I feel that all the nations that did not accept the Jews, at least temporarily, were equally guilty of their slaughter as was Hitler. This was the worst mass ethnic murder in the history of mankind.

Following the war, the few scattered remnants of Jews still alive in Europe sought refuge elsewhere to try to recover and start a new life. They fled to many countries but mainly to the USA and to Palestine to join the already-established Jewish community there. The British mandate force in Palestine tried valiantly to prevent the entry of the Jews there so as not to incur Arab wrath. The story of the ship The Exodus is well worth reading as it gives one an insight to the struggles of the Jews at the time to find a place to live on this planet. They were the world's unwanted ones, but there is no other planet.

By this time the British were sending Jewish immigrants to Cyprus and, seeing they could no longer restrain the interminable fighting between the Arabs and Jews, finally decided to relinquish the mandate. The United Nations agreed and the General Assembly approved the partition of Palestine into two separate, independent Arab and Jewish entities on November 29, 1947 generally based on land ownership and demographics. The Jews accepted the proposal. The Arabs rejected it out of hand without dialogue, negotiation or even the possibility of negotiation or compromise although much of the land reserved for the Jewish state had already been acquired though purchase by the Jews and had a Jewish majority. The Arabs called for a war of extermination against the Jews and seeing no alternative, military preparations were accelerated by both sides with inevitable clashes frequently occurring. By May 13, 1948 the British completed their evacuation of Palestine and lifted the blockade they had established thus allowing much-needed arms to enter Israel.

The next day the Jewish State of Israel was proclaimed in Tel Aviv and Dr. Chaim Weizmann was appointed as president with David Ben Gurion as prime minister. President Harry S. Truman of the United States immediately recognized Israel as a legitimate new state. The new Israeli government said it would grant full civil rights to all within its borders, whether Arab, Jew, Christian, Bedouin or Druze. The declaration stated: *We appeal to the Arab inhabitants of the State of Israel to preserve peace and participate in the upbuilding of the State on the basis of full and equal citizenship and due representation in all its provisional and permanent institutions.*

But having foreclosed any possibility of discussion, the Arabs were left with the only response they could muster: six Arab armies from neighboring states attacked the newborn Jewish state within hours of its formation. They spread word to the resident Arabs to flee lest they get caught in the ensuing war. Most fled to the "West Bank" (Judea and Samaria to the Jews) and Gaza areas controlled respectively by Jordan and Egypt. But a significant number remained in the territory of Israel and many, with their offspring, are still there to this day as Israeli citizens.

If anyone believes in miracles, it was surely one that saved Israel. A new country with only a ragtag volunteer defense force (consisting mostly of the Haganah militia with the Palmach, the Stern Gang and some Irgun) of highly motivated people with a magnificent fighting spirit defending their own lives and families with a hodgepodge of weapons and limited ammunition was somehow able to stave off disaster. That they did, routing the attacking armies with a vengeance to retain their partitioned area. It was very bloody but the Israelis won their land and remained in control of most of the area.

And so the Jewish state of Israel finally came into being: a bawling, screaming infant of a state. But it had a government, leadership, a language, money, a flag, postage stamps, and at least 2 billion enemies.

Had the Arabs accepted the United Nations partition plan, they would have had their "Palestinian homeland" for over 65 years by now. They spurned the opportunity when it was available to them. As the great Israeli statesman, Abba Eban, said years later following many such missed opportunities, "the Arabs never miss an opportunity to miss an opportunity". For nineteen years, until the Six-Day War in 1967, Jerusalem's Old City, the West Bank, and Gaza territories as well as the refugees within them were under the control of Jordan and Egypt. Neither country offered to accept their brethren into their home territory. Never during those years was there ever a demand for a "Palestinian homeland". Only after the Six-Day War when the territories reverted to Israeli control, did the insistent clamor for a "Palestinian" homeland arise. It is plausible to believe that, over the years, the surrounding Arab countries preferred to maintain and support the refugees under dreadful circumstances in camps as a means of promoting worldwide hate of the Jews and as a kind of local standing "army" to attack Israelis at will.

The Six-Day War was prompted by Gamal Abdel Nasser, leader of the United Arab Republic (at the time comprising Egypt, Syria, and Jordan) when he ordered a withdrawal of the United Nations Emergency Forces stationed on the Egyptian-Israeli border thus removing an international buffer. Moreover, the Arabs were widely publicizing the fact that they were amassing armies on Israel's borders for the purpose of finally exterminating Israel and its people. Realizing its perilous situation, the Israeli Airforce, in a preemptive strike on June 5th 1967, simultaneously attacked the U.A.R. airfields as well as those in Iraq which had joined the fray. Without dwelling on the complexities of reality, the military tactics, the intense suffering of people on both sides, and lives lost, the result of the war, which ended on June 10th, was the salvation of Israel which by then had captured Gaza, the West Bank, and east Jerusalem including the Old City.

All this is well known, researched and published history in the Western world. The Muslim world, however, does not even acknowledge all this nor even the legitimate existence of Israel. That entity does not appear on any of their maps, certainly not on the ones used in their schoolbooks ever or now. It is considered as Muslim territory occupied by infidels. Thus generations of their people are ignorant of the facts and totally brainwashed.

Just before the war began a young Egyptian came to the Arab West Bank to incite the people to rebel against the Israelis. His name was Yasser Arafat and he formed an organization called al Fatah with himself as leader. Later, in 1964, he helped found the P.L.O. (Palestinian Liberation Organization), a terrorist group with al Fatah as its chief military arm. Its aim was to destroy Israel and its Jewish inhabitants. And lo the Arab people thenceforth became Palestinians who proclaimed ownership of all the land including Israel.

Fast forward 39 years to 2005 during which time thousands of Israelis were slaughtered by Palestinian terrorists including the murders of Olympic athletes in Munich in 1972, numerous airline hijackings at Entebbe and Amman, the hijacking of the ship Achille Lauro, countless suicide bombings including the murder of several hundred American and French soldiers in Lebanon, the Intifadas, and on and on. At one time it got so bad that king Hussein of Jordan called upon Israel to help him expel Arafat and his al Fatah Palestinians from Jordan for fear of a takeover. Israel refused. In 1971 the usual trio of Egypt, Syria, and Jordan, unleashed a terrible unexpected war during the Jewish high holiday of Yom Kippur and almost succeeded in conquering Israel. With U.S. help (ammunition and equipment) they were thwarted. Israel vowed then never to be caught unprepared.

All this was perpetrated in full view and knowledge of the United States and world governments as well as the western media. Yet all consistently, in equal terms, described these events against Israelis as a round robin of attacks and retribution for previous attacks against Palestinians. No difference or true reason was ascribed to either side though Israel's response was concerned with security while the Palestinian concern was revenge and annihilation of Israel. The Islamic press, addressing 2 billion or so Muslims, naturally hailed every attack against Israel as a blessing. Nonetheless, the United States continued to provide foreign aid to Arafat, although at a lower level than that to Israel. Even the so-called Oslo accord in 1991 was a farce with Arafat being forced to acknowledge the existence of his bitter enemy, Israel. The Camp David meeting between Ehud Barak, prime minister of Israel, and Arafat under the aegis of President Bill Clinton in 1999 predictably ended in failure though Barak was willing to give Arafat about 95% of what he wanted (except Jerusalem). It was yet another example of the inability of Arabs to negotiate. It's their way or nothing. Arafat no doubt realized that his life was forfeit if he signed any paper with the Israeli government and, hence, didn't.

The foregoing is a light onceover of a very complex sequence of events that occurred in the Middle East over a period of a century. During this interval the U.S. seemed at times to be either uninterested, uncaring, unaware, a strong friend of Israel, a dubious enemy, a great provider of foreign aid, bewildered, and with a foreign policy seemingly dependent on its need for Middle East oil. Israel seemed to be just an abstraction in its many concerns.

Why should America be concerned with the struggles and strife among peoples in a small speck of land 7000 miles away?

It wasn't until the tragedy of 9/11 in 2001 occurred when, within hours, the World Trade Center and the Pentagon were attacked by hi-jacked airliners causing the loss of 3000 American lives. This suddenly prompted the United States to focus carefully to get to understand, even minimally, the violent terrorism that Israel had been enduring for decades. The airliners were hi-jacked by 19 Saudi Arabs.

Terrorism is not a local affair to be dealt with in situ. It is now worldwide in scope and may eventually include piracy at sea. Maybe the attacks hammered home some sense of the monstrousness of Muslim terror to the American people. I have doubts. What has Washington learned from all this? To attack Iraq? Afghanistan? Other? It appears to be flailing with no clear objective, methods or means.

As exemplified by the Palestinians, Muslims cannot live in peace together nor even speak the truth among themselves. By this time hate and terrorism are woven into their brain plasm and maybe even their DNA.

Can you believe, the American president, George W. Bush, invited Mahmoud Abbas, the leader of the Fatah branch of the Palestinian terrorists, to the White house on October 20, 2005 for policy discussions as if he were a world leader and promised him American help to control the Israelis? Was this the president's idea of neutrality? What kind of pretzel logic is that?

Consider the newly "liberated" Gaza strip from where several thousand Jews were evicted. It sprouted the Hamas authority whose prime objective is the obliteration of Israel and which directed thousands of rocket attacks on Israeli territory prompting immediate retaliation. It has become an overcrowded slum. The "Palestinian people" have ruined every single piece of land they have ever touched. They are among the biggest recipients of foreign aid in the world (from most of the Arab countries and even the USA) and what do they have to show for it? Modern schools and hospitals? Parks and playgrounds? A vibrant economy with high employment? No, just filthy streets, guns, bombs, and enough terrorist groups to fill a phone book. They import weapons and export terror. They teach their children hate and destruction and then sacrifice them to their "God of peace" as suicide bombers. They worship death and celebrate the murder of Israeli mothers and their babies. They danced in the streets after 9/11. They have never kept a single agreement they have ever signed. Even their Arab "brothers" hate their guts and will not allow them into their countries. Anyone who believes these people want peace or can be trusted in any way is simply delusional including some American and Israeli leaders.

Yet this is a potent moment in human history. A history that is essentially a prolonged continuum of competitive struggles between peoples for limited resources and power exacerbated by ignorance, stupidity, and organized religion. If we can understand and somehow resolve the complex issues in the Middle East such process could be applied to the world at large.

Although seemingly concerned with a minor piece of land, this struggle has much broader implications in that it is based on the teachings of the Qu'ran which forbids negotiation and dialogue while calling for the death of all infidels who do not share Muslim belief in it. This situation is serious enough to have engaged the entire world for years since it pits two major religions against each other and neither wants to listen to the other. But there is much to be said and heard because it concerns the well being of many people. Further, there is the ongoing education of hate and intolerance by Muslims that must be encouraged to stop. This may take a hundred years or more to accomplish to any significant degree but it must be started.

Today Saudi Arabia continues spending millions of dollars in the USA and elsewhere funding many schools, curricula, and materials to promote its hate campaign against the Jews and even Americans. It has done so for many years even after 9/11 because our laws allow it. We could take a leaf from their book in reverse and also not accept such propagandizing here. Isn't it strange that spreading truth among humans is among our most difficult tasks? We must help prevent or interdict the influx of weapons and money to the area. Since we consider ourselves the bearer of modernism, we must use the Internet, movies, television, and other communication techniques that we, in the West, have developed to rapidly outpace their lie dissemination capabilities. This will be very expensive and time consuming, but do we have an alternative? Very importantly, we must drastically reduce or eliminate our consumption of mid-east oil so at least we don't wind up paying for our demise. I am convinced that military intervention against suicide bombers is a never ending practice in frustration without surcease. But when the situation demands it, we must be prepared to use overwhelming force, well understood by the Arabs, to establish control and achieve useful objectives. What we have now cannot continue.

How can we implement a successful response? The situation remains that the Palestinians (and their foreign supporters) do not want to have a dialogue with the Israelis; rather their stated proximate policy is to destroy Israel and its people. To date no one has been able to dissuade them from that goal.

The key problem is the Qu'ran itself and its hold on the millions of Muslim people that follow it. This is further compounded by the continual provision of arms and funding to the Palestinians and other terrorists by all Muslim nations.

In response, the world of non-Muslim nations has a choice: do nothing and many thousands more people in the region and eventually the world at large will be killed in unprecedented waves of bloodshed with no settlement in sight; or figure out a response that will inhibit the cycle of hate and murder.

Working out any response through the United Nations is hopeless since the Arab nations there seem able to control its policies. Recall the resolution passed by the U.N. not long ago equating Zionism with Nazism? Outright military attack and attempts to establish democracy in Arab lands now is ludicrous and will only exacerbate conditions as seems to be the case in Iraq and Afghanistan.

Therefore, a cabal of western nations such as the European Union or NATO, the United States and some Asian countries must establish a common agenda to impose strict trade barriers and sanctions against nations that support Palestinian or Arab terrorism. This must include the interdiction of money and arms flowing to them. If not contained, this Arab terrorism will metastasize to include all of Europe, most of Asia and will directly threaten the United States in short order.

The West must establish an overwhelming system of education and communication with the Muslim community worldwide in scope to slow and inhibit the flow of inflammatory propaganda to its people. The response must be dynamic in that it must change with conditions and increase as the situation warrants. It is conceivable that the Qu'ran may have to undergo some modification by Muslims to enable peaceful coexistence with non-Muslims. Otherwise the world must be prepared to deal with Arab hostility continuously for many years, perhaps a century or more, with the hope of reducing that hostility.

Peace only comes with mutual understanding, but how can you have understanding without reasoned discussion or debate?

If the Jews and the Palestinians ever learn to live in peace together they will both harvest the rich rewards the area can provide.

CHAPTER 14

The Who Versus the What

*But men may construe things, after their fashion,
clean from the purpose of the things themselves*

– from *Julius Caesar* by William Shakespeare

MANY TIMES, THE labeling of who is saying something
deflects the listener from the substance of what is being
said, particularly in the political arena. Legions of "spin
doctors" are engaged and millions of dollars are expend-
ed to ensure that this is so. Nowadays simply calling a
person a liberal by adversarial groups is sufficient to
taint every word spoken by that individual to the point
where any wisdom uttered is promptly disregarded. The
same may be true for a person labeled a conservative.
Obviously little is learned by name-calling especially
when it is indiscriminately applied and the labels themselves are ill-understood. Issues are never clarified by
mud-slinging. We should at least have a good idea of the

background of who is doing the name-calling. Therefore we try to define here in clear form the salient features of the two key political ideologies, conservatism and liberalism, currently popular in the U.S. as understood by many mature residents.

Conservatism

1. Republican party conservatism espouses the Darwinian principle of the survival of the fittest which in secular economic terms means "survival of the most powerful or wealthiest" individuals at the expense of the less fortunate – a true zero-sum game. Corollary: people are not equal(ly endowed) and so those who are smarter, drive themselves harder, work more and harder, and are more fortunate, deserve more. Frequently, this leads to initiative and innovation.

2. By definition, such conservatism is bereft of compassion (as is nature) and therefore it does not and cannot have or espouse any significant social agenda involving issues such as universal public education, arts endowment for the public, universal health care, economic support for the elderly and infirm, affordable shelter, environmental protection, national parks, etc.. Instead, voluntary private philanthropy is expected to fund many of these social needs. It seeks to conserve, maintain, and protect the personal wealth and status of certain individuals against the claims and inroads of external forces.

3. Conservatives raise the question of whether government at all levels should be expected to provide equal services to all citizens when the taxes collected from each citizen are not equal but done on a graduated basis of income and property, and some do not pay any taxes at all.

4. Conservatives believe that it is wrong for government to mandate by taxation or other means (in their terms) the confiscatory redistribution of wealth from the industrious and talented to the indolent, ignorant, indigent and even criminal elements of society. (By criminal is meant the huge expense of prisons and the overly tolerant criminal- justice system -- perhaps more aptly named the victim-justice system – and the under-application of capital punishment). And don't burn any flags!

5. "Individual effort should yield individual rewards" is generally viewed as a conservative philosophy not espoused by workers' unions.

6. Conservatives generally shy away from the enactment of social legislation for the benefit of the populace at large and seek to undo any social reform that somehow occurred before their time (ie., social security, medicare, affirmative action, etc.) to the extent of "whatever the traffic will bear".

7. In the event of an economic downturn, conservatives are generally in favor of subsidizing businesses and reducing taxation of the wealthy

in the hope that eventually such money will "trickle down" to the public at large and thereby energize the economy.

8. When conservatives team up with right wing religious groups as is usually the case, you can be sure that planned parenthood and unfettered biological research are in jeopardy. Moreover, they consistently urge religious prayer in schools as well as government, though which religion to formally adopt has not quite yet been finalized into law.

9. Conservative foreign policy follows a distinct America first approach with minor regard for the attitudes of other nations. That policy may disregard worldwide environmental and social considerations. As a result, a strong military force must be created and sustained to serve as a bulwark against external intrusion and possible offensive action.

Liberalism

1. The key feature of liberalism is its belief in equal opportunity for all and its concern for social issues. They consider a society defective when it promotes the same goals for everyone without giving all equal access to achieve them.

2. Social concerns and agenda should include: health, energy, environmental protection, banking, auto and air safety, education, the civil service system, taxation, scientific research, antitrust policy, work

safety, public transportation, roads, public recreation, support of the arts, justice, the possibility to reform, freedom, opportunity, sufficient police to ensure public tranquillity, and so on.

3. Liberals are concerned with what is best for the most. This conflicts at times with the well-being of the wealthiest in our society.

4. In the event of an economic downturn, liberals are generally in favor of directly subsidizing the unemployed and poor by unemployment insurance and/or tax relief so more people will have more money sooner to buy things and thereby stimulate the economy.

5. Liberals do not usually espouse the integration of religious activities in public schools, government, scientific research and planned-parenthood.

6. The promulgation of social legislation such as social security, minimum wage, and medicare usually occurs under liberal auspices.

7. Liberal regimes generally try to maintain friendly, or at least talking relationships with foreign governments to the greatest extent while working through the United Nations organization. This approach usually tends to reduce the need for an extensive military buildup. Therefore, military expenditures, while sufficient for defense, are usually balanced with national social needs.

So when liberals and conservatives give each other the finger you now know who it is that's doing the pointing.

CHAPTER **15**

Education for Parents

If you can't state the problem, you will never find the solution.

–L.S.

IT TOOK A long time to create the educational pickle we're in today. It seems we can't afford the cost of educating our children which is getting more expensive with each passing year. And if we don't change our funding methodology now, you can expect that sooner or later we'll have to borrow educational funds from the very children we're trying to educate. To continue raising these funds the same way we've done for generations by taxing non-income producing residential property plus some minimal government trinkets and expecting some eventual change to ease the funding problem is tantamount to insanity defined as doing the same thing over and over again and expecting change. Like always planting peanuts and hoping to eventually harvest tomatoes.

We need to reinvent the way we think about creating a sustainable, more affordable method of educating children on a nationwide and local basis. Initially, of course, we must establish national and state priorities to rank order our needs in terms of health care, military requirements, education, social security, environmental concerns, and the like. Paying for all these is constrained by the GDP we produce each year which is then divided among the competing component needs in accordance with their ranked importance. Once the budget or percentage for education is determined, we must work within that figure at all government levels. This may also cause us to determine how many kids we can educate adequately within that figure.

Setting aside the issue of scholastic achievement, which I think we can all agree should be the highest level the kids can attain, three key issues are tearing asunder the very fabric of our educational process in the United States. They are:

- Teachers' salaries
- Number of children to be educated
- Funding source and amount.

The issue of the number of our children undergirds and drives the two others.

It doesn't take a rocket scientist or a housewife to perceive that reducing the number of children for a given number of parents can ease the salary and funding problems. For instance, if 100 parents bring 50 kids instead of 200 for enrollment in a school system, things become quite affordable for those parents. Unfortunately, rather than constrain the number of children to be educated, parents and the society they form have figured out over the years how to sidestep this issue by legally allocating a large portion of the cost of educating their offspring to people (seniors, for instance) and organizations that have nothing to do with the school system. This, of course, shifts the burden of funding away from the parents and hence invites larger broods per couple to be educated thereby requiring a greater degree of alternate funding and so on. The problem cycle is thus complete. And don't tell seniors that since the education of their children was paid for by others the same process should continue indefinitely. A break with that stupidity has to begin at some point and that time is now, the sooner the better.

Teachers and education leaders are caught in the midst of this vexing problem--: increase the number of teachers to deal with the ever-growing army of children or teach more kids per class and then hope and fight on a perennial basis for a larger salary and facilities to cope with this issue. Since the funding resource doesn't grow as fast as the number of children, the teaching difficulties are endlessly exacerbated. Though most visible in the education sector, the inability of one generation to pay for the folly of the past while simultaneously trying to pay for the needs of the next generation in all aspects of society are made clearly evident by the heavy borrowing pursued by the government and its people to meet debt obligations (now sitting at over $12 trillion in the U.S. with over 300 million inhabitants). Maybe we are already borrowing from our children.

The People's Republic of China, with a population of over one billion people, recognized a generation ago the root cause of their seemingly never-ending cyclic circumstance of debt and poverty and instituted a law limiting the number of children per family to one. At the time China was subjected to ridicule and accused of heartlessness by churches and states but did not change the law. Today China is reaping the reward for its foresight. Children could be well educated at affordable cost and many jobs were waiting for them when they graduated. The end result being the greatest economic boom China has ever experienced. Can we learn from this? We had better—after all China, with its foreign exchange reserves, owns a significant portion of the U.S. national debt in the form of government bonds and other instruments. At this point it sounds like a good idea to start learning Chinese.

At the other end of the education spectrum is the continent of Africa where families are so large and children so numerous (they are effectively the parents' social security in old age) that getting any education is a hit or miss proposition. Nearly all higher education is achieved off-continent for a very few lucky ones. Education seems to be considered a low priority need in Africa and, without controlled parenthood and sufficient investment from external sources, Africa is doomed to third world status in perpetuity.

In a recent book *Freakanomics,* authors Steven D. Levitt and Stephen J, Dubner linked falling crime rates to legalized abortion of unwanted babies which produced fewer criminals twenty or so years later. This is difficult to prove but the concept bears consideration. None can deny that the first places where problems caused by a surfeit of children show up are in obstetrics departments and public schools. That's where differences in intellectual capability and achievement are first recognized in an organized and measurable way.

Education is the factory that turns animals into human beings. Late computer technology introduced as part of the educational process is mitigating its cost and the challenge of making kids smart. But the real meaningful improvement will come about when planned-parenthood becomes a widespread way of life. Society's top priority should be to ensure that the best education is equally available to all its children so as to sustain and enhance itself. Let us therefore make sure that the funding and perpetuation of education is secure.

CHAPTER **16**

The Me versus the We

True capitalism is bereft of social conscience

– LS

ﻭﻭﻭ

The benefit of the many is rarely so for the individual

– LS

LET'S FACE IT, on this oblate spheroid called earth there isn't enough to go around comfortably for everyone (or even every organism). There never was or will be. If the past is any guide we're faced with a constant battle of survival amongst ourselves forevermore. And that's so whether things are somehow equally distributed or not. And they never will be. It will get tougher henceforth because the earth refuses to grow in proportion with human proliferation. It will be the ultimate test of Darwinian survival principles.

With all the intellectual brilliance we have demonstrated to ourselves, we still do not seem to have figured out a way to contain the massive hordes of people visible to any worldwide traveler. Overpopulation is the root cause of poverty, war and almost every other problem. Where once this was mainly a Chinese-Indian problem in far off Asia, it now afflicts the entire globe. Nearly every major national capital in the world today has 10 to 20 million inhabitants and growing. Half the people in the world today live in cities. To boot, the procreation rate is highest where the people are poorest and have the least ability to support themselves. Many religions support and even demand fruitful multiplication presumably to gain or maintain power. But is it really fruitful for humanity overall? Is it the lot of us humans, in chasing for scraps to survive, to be destined to live in perpetual discontent, corruption, and war? Can we ever look forward to a time of peace and contentment? Yes, if we first learn to curtail our numbers, overcome our mean instincts and frailties, and adhere to a consistent set of just laws and sensible economic principles to live by. Every intelligent adult on this planet and every nation knows what to do to contain or reduce population so there is no excuse for not addressing this problem head-on.

I've come to the realization that the number of people occupying any given area of land should not exceed the ability of that land to support them in reasonable comfort. When that number is exceeded, basic requirements such as water, food, energy (trees, fossil fuel or electricity) and the like must be brought in or made available from elsewhere to those people. Further, trash removal and air and water pollution must be dealt with at great expense. This is, in effect, the definition of a city. Cities, of course, offer the benefit of employment opportunity, the arts, museums, the latest fashions, and many conveniences available in close proximity. But at a substantial price. At some point this price may be deemed too high to pay for a city's blessings.

One of the most impressive achievements of modern civilization, in its attempt to overcome a paucity of and need for redistribution of resources and goods, is the rise of *economic* capitalism and of *political* socialism (populism) as means of addressing society's survival needs. In my view, both are simultaneously necessary to yield a stable society; but when each is applied singly while excluding the other, either uncontrolled economic swings or stultification arise which cause great distress to most of the people sharing that societal form. People seem to think the two are somehow incompatible and are generally viewed as being inimical to each other but they are not. Yet when one or the other is missing in governmental structure as in the Soviet Union of yore (no capitalism) and substantially in the United States of today (hardly any socialism) dire consequences result as history attests. Wealthy capitalists and right wing economists are blinded and get dyspeptic at the mere notion and concept of socialism while socialists and their far-left communist brethren view capitalism as a curse or nothing better than a lottery. This is most unfortunate since both, working together, can offer greater benefits than each alone. Economic stability must be approached on the basis of duality: personal needs and social needs. *The me versus the we.* One enhances *wealth* while the other enhances *well-being.* The difficulty in addressing this issue is the unwillingness of government leaders to accept the concept of conflating the two to obtain one steady-state economic way of life that satisfies the most people. Further, politicians often disregard the public interest because the public is frequently unaware of what that interest is.

Yes, capitalism exemplifies personal greed with all its faults, but at the same time accentuates the human need to build, innovate, be daring, and beat everyone else at the game whatever it happens to be. It has produced great technological revolutions in industrial, informational and communication fields the fruits of which we are enjoying today. The drive for wealth, power and comfort is undeniably a powerful force that in some ways is the human world system expression of the principle of Darwinian survival. Nonetheless, it should not be a gamble. People have a right to expect a connection between effort and reward (not a roll of the dice) or life becomes apparently arbitrary and brutal. That's what makes capitalism so wrenching sometimes. It cares not a whit beyond the few who stand to profit from some artfully devised schemes for fleecing their own labor force and the gullible public. I'm talking here about major corporations that form the foundation of the capitalist system not the myriad small business merchants, mom-and-pop stores and even individuals that abound all over, even in communist China, ready to buy or sell anything. How can a system, whose

very existence is based on the idea that personal success is measured only by attained wealth with its derived
power from the exploitation and sacrifice of everyone and
everything else—essentially a zero sum game between
the haves and have-nots---be considered a desirable economic way of life? After all, look around you and note
that capitalism, in and of itself, is devoid of social conscience or social relevance. As the embodiment of private
free enterprise it does not, never has been able to, and
cannot be expected to provide a social safety net for all
its participants in the form of public education, welfare,
health care, environmental protection, assurance of the
availability of potable water, social security for the elderly
and handicapped, the arts, and much else.

The intelligentsia among us have commented on
capitalism's value and social void, occasionally finding difficulty establishing a personal position on it.
Daniel Bell in his book "The Cultural Contradictions
of Capitalism", 1978, says he is a socialist in economics, a liberal in politics, and a conservative in culture.
Alternatively, in "Slouching Toward Gommorah: Modern
Liberalism and American Decline" Robert Bork unequiv-
ocally states that "our commitment to equality keeps
bumping violently into the natural order of things, which
is hierarchical". He says "don't question the triumphs of
the proficient over the slow, rich over the poor, men over
women, whites over blacks, Western culture over everyone else". Sounds like the ultimate description of right
wing capitalism, which it is, and what one could expect
from such a regime.

It has been said that capitalism and its free markets have brought unprecedented prosperity to the greatest number of people ever. It may have but, unfortunately, it isn't a steady-state, ubiquitous blessing. From time to time it goes through extended periods of panics, recessions, depressions, and general convulsions that cause misery and hardship to most people living under its economic benevolence. Some of this cyclical instability is undoubtedly caused by financial speculation as opposed to productive investment, the principal driving force behind business. Moreover, speculative capital flow, based on the existence of market instability, has the effect of disorganizing all steady business thus prompting the need for control or regulation of capital movements nationally and for international investments according to a major economist, John Maynard Keynes. He reasoned that capitalism, if left to its own devices, is chronically unstable. Based on that premise, capital flow intended for business around the world today is closely controlled by law and agreed upon rules. Though mitigating extreme business swings, this approach has so far not been able to produce the steady-state stable economic climate we're all looking for.

No society can exist for long under raw, unadulterated capitalism because in its actualization much of the public is excluded from the benefits of its created wealth except, perhaps minimally, by the so-called trickle-down effect. Even Adam Smith, Ayn Rand, and Milton Friedman, all well-known advocates of pure capitalism, conceded to some of its inadequacies and the need for minor limited control. Free markets and investment (money supply), if left completely to their own devices by a laisser-faire system, becomes a conspiracy of producers against consumers, of sellers against buyers and can wind up terribly unfree by virtue of monopolistic tendencies. (Think price-fixing and gouging by oil companies.) Friedman himself said that whenever men of the same trade meet they conspire against the public.

In a crazy way, if monopolies are allowed to merge and grow without restraint to the size of a national government you automatically have a communist regime where the entire population becomes workers for the state monopoly at a low wage led by a well-off junta. This brings us around full circle. Sound familiar? Some of these outfits can grow to extra-national size on the global stage beyond control of any one government. It seems to be happening already. The concept of a totally free market unregulated by forces external to it (such as governments) being able to run itself stably to the benefit of consumers as well as the business participants is pure bunk. Even diehard conservatives who decry government intrusion into private business activities must bear witness with considerable despair to the need for government bailout of airlines (after 9/11), passenger rail carriers (always), automobile manufacturers such as GM and Chrysler during the recent recession, hospitals (natural and man-made catastrophes), banks, insurance companies like AIG (plus emergencies like Katrina and forest fires with FEMA) and others. Additionally,

government bears responsibility for determining locations for disposal of nuclear waste, political disposition
of foreign commerce, and much more.

However, one must acknowledge an important positive concept and benefit that capitalism has given us that
applies to any endeavor: nothing gets done or should
get done unless it is beneficial or profitable and can be
measured as such. The positive and negative attributes
of capitalism are so well known and have been experienced and studied by so many over centuries that any
further observation is now so obvious as to be banal.

But what of socialism? Its very name implies primary
consideration of the public weal followed by that for the
individual. Under socialism each of us is being asked
to do something beneficial for all of us, while some of
us feel that what may be best for all of us is not best
for each of us. It's that simple. It's that difficult and becoming more so with rising population. Remember, the
United States constitution does not dictate the form of
economic regime the country must have nor does it ex-
clude any. We are free to choose from the gamut of right
wing capitalism all the way through to left wing com-
munism. Americans seem to have settled on fractured
capitalism with just enough social handouts to prevent
uprisings. History tells us that private enterprise, which
owes its very existence to public support, i.e. purchasing power, cannot be depended on to address the social
needs of the public.

Many feel that socialism, taken to its extreme, implies
that everyone gets equal low pay and services regardless

of one's ability or contribution to society. It simply isn't so. It's just recognition that people worry about health care and insurance, retirement and social security, care for aging parents, paying for public education, income and property taxes, sending kids to college, job security, affordable housing, honest elections, and holding elected officials accountable. These are important common concerns and needs that all of us have to deal with that cannot be disregarded by any compassionate society. Indeed, there is a psychological boost in knowing that we're in the same worry boat together contributing to the welfare of all by forming, in a sense, a mutually supportive societal group. We are all interdependent and getting more so with our growing numbers. The days of singular self-reliance are gone. Even our money says "e pluribus unum", from the many, one. This should not be misconstrued to mean that we're all supposed to contribute by toil and sweat to the benefit of a single individual or cabal.

As I said at the outset of this chapter, there isn't enough to go around equally and comfortably for everyone. If some take more from the common well of resources (labor and nature) others, of necessity, must have less. So, figuratively, the horizon of incomes in the United States now is very hilly with a few very tall peaks scattered about surrounded by a vast expanse of deep valleys. It is not possible or desirable to create or even envision an economic system with a totally smooth income horizon that can, over the long haul, assure an equal distribution of wealth. All we can hope to do is reduce the disparity somewhat between maximum and minimum incomes. And there's the rub: we should really be concerned with some constraint on a *maximum* income in addition to establishing a minimum wage. Aside from differences over foreign policy, social security, and congressional rules, that's the predominant reason why our two main political parties keep bumping into each other and are at continuous loggerheads. The battle lines are forming now all over the world in every major country, including the United States, to prevent by any means possible the redistribution of wealth from the haves to the have-nots by means of more fair-share progressive taxation and maximum income constraint. So far there are no cracks in the defense wall, the wealthy seem to be winning. This is not new. We've been on this merry-go-round before for over a century in the United States when the industrial revolution was in full swing. Remember child labor, the time before federal income tax, before anti-trust laws, the Molly Maguires of the mines, the Haymarket riots, the constant battles for unionization with head cracking and murder, the formation of the AFL and CIO. These were the bitterly fought early min-max income disparity battles and they're still in progress. One party wants to get rid of any constraint on maximum incomes (by re-ducing or even eliminating their income tax), while the other is trying to increase the legal minimum wage and if it could, restore or increase the progressive income tax on high incomes to partially subsidize social needs. Let's not have social amnesia and replay that century-old game again but progress from there. Further, I think it's high time to realize that the promulgation of an economically stable society involves the concept of a necessary perpetual overhead of about 16% of our GDP devoted to the support of our less fortunate members, who by age, illness, or handicap, prevents them from becoming full profitable contributors to our wherewithal. That or triage.

Moreover, the American public clamors for some governmental support for key social needs which are not now being sufficiently addressed such as health care and education. Expenditures in these social areas should be viewed as high-return investments rather than social welfare payments because a healthy, educated public will always yield a big GDP payback.

In case you think this is blue sky, there is precedent for this on-going for many years in Scandinavian countries. They are advanced industrial nations and doing just fine. Their economic data challenge widespread American economic beliefs – for instance, that high taxes stifle business. Sweden and Denmark have the first and second highest income tax burden in the capitalist world, roughly double those of the United States. But consider the following Denmark data:

- It has the highest living standard in the world
- It exports more goods and services than it imports
- Unemployment is a stable 3.1%
- Corporate taxes are lower than in the United States
- It provides free education

- It provides free health care
- If you lose your job, the government provides you up to 90% of earnings for at least 4 years plus retraining if needed
- 76% of respondents to recent polls think that globalization is a good thing.

But there are no super-rich folks there. I think their biggest concern is maintaining sobriety during long, dark winter nights. We ought to take a few pages from their book.

There will always be tension between private initiative and public purpose, but they should not be mutually exclusive. Either is harmed when the other is not present. Ultimately, greed should not be the decisive and defining factor.

I believe capitalism and socialism should be complementary strands in a stable society's economic structure. The goal, now as ever, is not to choose one over the other or to blur the distinction between them. Instead it should be to weave them together in the right combination so that they reinforce each other for the benefit of all the people.

CHAPTER 17

Cosmic Thoughts

HAVE YOU EVER wondered about the progress and timing of life's important episodes from birth through old age of not only us humans but of all mammals and creatures on this planet? Yes, we now know all about genetic DNA and quite recently its switches and timers, but there must be an additional mechanism that clocks the time for baby teeth loss, the time for puberty, the time for growth and growth stoppage, the time for gray hair and/or hair loss, the time for various changes in our senses over the years, and finally the time for our physical decay. I do not think that DNA, in and of itself, is sufficient to program life's sequential functions over a period of years. It does superbly well during gestation but after birth the rate of progress must be triggered by forces external to the DNA. In short-lived creatures such as a fruit fly, its entire life is probably pre-determined by the DNA itself at birth.

We cannot rationally presume ourselves on this

planet to be floating totally unperturbed in the universe devoid of all interaction to the myriad other celestial bodies with their cumulative gravitational and radiation effects. I propose that our genetic process is timed by a constant and consistent high energy particle shower and/or bombardment emanating from galactic and extra-galactic sources (super novas, black holes, etc.). This particle energy is of such great magnitude that it permeates all organic matter as well as, to a lesser extent, the full earth itself. The existence of high energy ionizing radiation external to the earth itself and the solar system was first postulated about a century ago. Victor Hess, an Austrian-American physicist, first measured such radiation in 1912 using a balloon to raise his detector to a significant altitude (about 2 miles) to measure it. The existence of this radiation has been confirmed by numerous and more accurate measurements since then.

Since we earthly creatures have developed to our present state of being over many millennia on the same planet we currently live on, it is reasonable to assume that during such a long development period organisms, including humans and other mammals, have completely adjusted to the continuous presence of a high energy particle shower as well as solar and earthly radiations much as we have adjusted to and thrive in the chemical composition of the air we breathe. Our DNA has altered or inured itself to accept this shower as a means of establishing a clock for its normal extended time functions including the time for an organism's eventual demise. Cosmic particles from beyond the solar system can have energies up to many millions of electron volts, far higher than gamma radiation or that created by man-made particle accelerators. Our sun also emits a significant level of cosmic energy associated with solar flares much of which frequently corrupts electronic device operation. All this energy impinges on the earth's upper atmosphere and its magnetic field which protect us. The residual energy (comprising pions, kaons, mesons, and muons and some other ionizing particles according to physicists) which eventually strikes all living matter on the earth's surface in a sufficient quantity to affect DNA is mostly secondary radiation from the atmosphere as well as some primary penetrating particles. That such cosmic radiation is serious business has been the basis of decade-long studies by NASA of its effects on the health and aging of astronauts whose space flights take them away from the partially protective cover of the earth's atmosphere.

Cosmic energy flux is believed to remain constant, though recent research shows an approximate 1.5 to 2 fold change over millennial time scales in the past 40,000 years which is exceedingly slow relative to mammalian lifetimes.

Particles with higher energy than gamma rays (x-rays) might be less harmful because the body is relatively transparent to them. Mammalian cells can provide limited repair of the breaking of DNA strands due to x-rays but perhaps not to cosmic radiation.

It is now settled fact that the number of x-rays a person receives in life produces a cumulative deleterious biological effect on the body which at some point may lead to a proclivity to some forms of cancer or other potential terminal illness. In recognition of such effect, x-ray radiation levels used for skeletal imaging have been decreased by design in recent decades to forestall or reduce the possible onset of forms of cancer, a seeming admission of measurable effect. This is indicative of the high sensitivity of the human body, particularly its DNA, to external radiation. As in cancer development, minute radiation-caused changes in our DNA could affect its clocking mechanism.

Though cosmic particles at much higher energy level than that used for imaging x-rays pass through the body, they occur at a low continuous rate compared to a relatively infrequent higher level sudden pulse-burst of gamma rays to produce images. These particles arrive at a rate of about 200 per square meter each second all the time and the DNA presumably responds to that. Medical x-rays now account for about 10% of total radiation exposure in the United States. Late scientific investigation seems to indicate that cancer arises at the most basic cellular element in the body, its DNA. One can then ask if conquering cancer is indeed within the realm of possibility if we spend every moment of our entire lives under the influence of cosmic radiation over which we have no control or capability of escaping. There is good reason to believe that there is great variability in the sensitivity of the DNA of one person to the next to cosmic radiation which may explain why various forms of cancer strike different individuals randomly at any age from infancy through old age and why this disease as well as others like Parkinson's and Alzheimer's are yielding so slowly to all our efforts to thwart them.

People's tumors may harbor thousands of genetic mutations or abnormalities unique to the specific individuals where they originated and thus each may react differently to the radiation that strikes them at any time and to the treatment provided. New scientific investigations seem to indicate that cancers may vary from one person to the next and that broad based treatments for all with a single class of drugs may be less beneficial than a specific drug tailored for a certain type of tumor for a specific individual. However, this puzzling individualized cancer occurrence may be a good indication of the existence of external causes such as cosmic radiation coupled with our ever-changing and growing inhaled and ingested pollution.

Recent research on telomeres – pieces of DNA that cap chromosomes – indicates that telomeres in aging cells start to shrink over time limiting eventually the cell's capability to reproduce itself. It seems all new research keeps uncovering biological time-counting mechanisms of the DNA that may indeed track the external radiation level over a limited singular lifetime to solve the riddle of 'when' should things happen.

So are we each destined to wear out like a threadbare coat with little hope of a longer happy life because of where we live? Stay tuned.

Carrying the cosmic proposition of DNA timing and morphing within a lifetime several steps forward, it is not inconceivable that cosmic, extra-terrestrial radiation may play a vital role in the mutation of species over a period of thousands or millions of years. The work of Charles Darwin and other like-minded scientists dealt with the survival and origin of species as being related to long term physical changes in the local environments which eventually produce species mutation. In his day, the existence of DNA and its attributes was totally unknown. So his thesis was based entirely on the effects of terrestrial environmental causes.

Today, however, we can measure and understand, perhaps in an as yet limited way, how a creature's genome, comprised of thousands of DNA sequences, specifies fundamentally and thoroughly what that creature is and isn't. It defines the very nature of what we are as organisms: humans, apes, cats, ants, fish, oak trees, amoebas, etc. and even specific individuals of a given species. And every species known is one of nature's myriad experiments in devising all manner of life to fill all the niches of existence possible on earth.

This experimentation is an ongoing process that started when the earth was formed billions of years ago, continues to this very day, and will continue indefinitely. During this time period the earth's environment has changed immensely and so have the organisms and their DNA that have evolved and disappeared over that long stretch of time as archeological evidence attests.

We can infer now that major changes to DNA sequences sufficient to cause significant alteration in the bearer's appearance and behavior occur very slowly over millions of years. Aside from occasional tsunamis, meteor strikes, fitful earthquakes at unpredictable locations the only constant external force over many epochs remains cosmic radiation. Droughts, floods, and famines which encourage mass migration or its equivalent may affect, in the short term of millennia, say between ice ages, noticeable changes to ways-of-life and appearance.

It takes millions of years of DNA mutation including that due to cosmic radiation to make life forms appear or disappear or morph into radically different species or groups of sub-species. It may be that some of the DNA sequences in a genome, now termed 'DNA junk', may be left over detritus from earlier forms of today's creatures.

This should be of great interest to those doing research in the field of bio-archeology trying to formulate causes and timing for the mutation of organisms.

CHAPTER **18**

How Fast Is Time?

ALTHOUGH WE MEASURE time by agreed-upon consistent means so we can watch TV shows and meet each other on some schedule, time does not always seem to flow at the same rate to all people all the time. To a small baby, a week is a lifetime. To a child, two months of school seems endless while for vacation, the same two months race by in an eyeblink. In mid-life our multi-year career workloads seem to persist timelessly without end.

But at retirement age, time really flies by at the quickest pace imaginable and indeed even assumes entirely new dimensions:

- A year comprises only two months---a cold one and a warm one.
- Each month seems to be only a week long.
- A week has only two days---a weekday and a weekend day, if you can tell the difference.

- A day consists of two hours---one of dark, the other of light.
- An hour is now only ten minutes.

And then you're another year older.

CHAPTER 19

The Future Is Past

AS AGE CREEPS up, one senses that the future seems to be crushing down on the ephemeral now with increasing rapidity. In earlier years things happened in time windows of months and years, later in weeks and today in milliseconds. The age of efficiency is over. This is the age of immediacy, faster than the speed of thought. A week is an eternity, yesterday is ancient.

Soon the future may overtake the present and we will inevitably live in the future without having experienced the pleasures of now. We will be part of a futuristic vintage and there will be museums of the future.

Now I'll have to start writing this chapter which you have just read.

CHAPTER **20**

Out of the Well

The average man's judgment is so poor, he runs a risk every time he uses it

– E.W. Howe

IT'S ALL AROUND us if we just pause long enough to try to make sense out of this turbulent world. Here are mostly my unchanging truisms accumulated over a lifetime's first-hand experience that should not be overlooked and which apply to much of our every day concerns. They seem to be self-evident.

- We can't afford ourselves
- Money begets money faster than labor
- If you can't state the problem you will never find the solution
- Our dietetic needs for survival simultaneously promote our eventual demise

- Organized religion is mankind's biggest self-invented curse
- When ignorance reigns, religion flourishes and vice versa
- True capitalism is bereft of social conscience
- Wealth is only created by labor
- Repeated taxation of assets is never a good idea (such as property tax)
- If you don't learn you will repeat your blunders
- Horseshit pervades humanity
- The most expensive commodities that people can possess are time, pride, and compassion
- Humanity is committing mass suicide by befouling the earth with its unbridled hordes and activities
- There is no such thing as enlightened self-interest
- The benefit of the many is rarely so for the individual
- In any organization garbage always floats to the top and shit rolls downhill
- Illegal immigration in the 21st century is akin to slavery before the Civil War
- Our main essence of life, the sun, is also our biggest killer (UV, melanoma, cosmic rays, drought)
- There is no such thing as competitive pricing in the marketplace of life's necessities (ie., power, potable water, public education, health care, shelter, living space)
- Competence does not appear to be a necessary qualification for public office

- Those who lie to get elected to public office should not be allowed to attain that office
- Ignorance contains its own shield against enlightenment
- Stupidity is ignorance compounded
- Religion and emotion are the enemies of rational thought
- Speak the truth but leave immediately after
- Technology alone is not enough; we must also engage with our hearts
- Higher productivity for one may mean unemployment for another
- Individualism must be mitigated or cease when it threatens the legitimate, shared concerns of the community
- Leisure begets philosophy
- History proves that war is better at abolishing nations than nations are at abolishing war
- You can fool *all* the people *all* the time if the advertising is right and the budget is big enough
- Organized religion blinds the eye and dulls the mind
- Global warming is an outgrowth of global stupidity; cure one – cure the other
- The only way to get rich is with other people's money
- Politics, like religion, is usually a family legacy
- Education is the factory that turns animals into human beings
- There will always be tension between the ME and

the WE (where ME means individual self-interest and WE means collective interests)
- Live within your means or you will have to live without your means
- Some people do nothing so nicely it appears to become something; learn to recognize that sham
- Remember you can only learn while listening, not talking
- Property tax is a virulent form of home-icide

Epilogue

SO WHO ARE we? As the fleeting primordial dust of the universe, yet with spirit and feeling, we are the captives of our genes: the physical, mental, temperamental, wildly idiosyncratic, sociable, personable, loving, hating, artistic, tragic, destructive, beautiful and sometimes horrible manifestations of our genetic inheritance. And any attempt to override these traits is bound to wind up as mostly wasted effort. Our meager efforts at constraining our genetic tendencies by environmental suppression such as education, social training, active sports (possibly as a substitute for war or the like), traditions, customs, religions and the rest can accentuate or palliate our inborn propensities but generally have been as mildly effective as a baby pacifier. The continued existence of prisons, war, and terrorism as a long term human legacy attest to their inadequacy.

Tampering directly with our DNA as we are doing experimentally today is tantalizing but fraught with dangers as well as potential blessings. Unfortunately the time window needed to assess the success or failure of these endeavors is measured in millennia not months. We had better tread very gently and carefully in this garden.

So it may be that as long as humanity persists there will always be, as there always has been, a continuing struggle between good and evil. Perhaps the real struggle in this world may be more optimistically viewed as one between hope and evil. Hope seems more active and creative than the somewhat nebulous good. At least it seems to portend some sort of future existence with the potential of an ameliorated society. Yet ultimately, after the last "good/evil" combatants perish, who will remain to assess the final human legacy? There is a passage from I Corinthians in which Paul says "the last enemy that shall be destroyed is death".

Perhaps we should stop worrying about the end of civilization. Maybe it wasn't such a good idea in the first place. When all is said and done, all the folly and wisdom of man will be overwhelmed by the forces of nature.

"What fools (most of) these mortals be!"

– with homage to W. Shakespeare
(from *A Midsummer Night's Dream*)

CPSIA information can be obtained at www.ICGtesting.com
Printed in the USA
BVOW042147100413

317856BV00008B/243/P

9 781478 716549